Developing Fiction Skills

John Jackman   Wendy Wren

Nelson

Contents

Unit	DEVELOPMENT	SKILLS	
	Text	Word	
1 Homes	A Home for Grandfather	Synonyms	Adding 'ing'
2 Fairy Stories	Hansel and Gretel	Synonyms	Prefix 'un'
3 Animal Homes	The Mice Who Lived in a Shoe	Synonyms – 'said'	'i-e' and 'igh' letter patterns
4 Weather	'Winter Morning' and 'Snow'	Using a dictionary	'ow' letter pattern
5 Animals	Animal Tales	Letter order	Comparing words
6 Magic	Merlin	Antonyms	Silent letters
7 Mazes	Theseus and the Minotaur	Using a dictionary	Contractions
8 Hands	A Poem About Hands	Using a thesaurus	Adding 'ing'
9 Parties	The Mad Hatter's Tea Party	Synonyms – 'said'	Contractions
10 Storms	The Cyclone	Homonyms	Singular and plural nouns
11 Books	Book Reviews	Homonyms	Root words
12 Tea	I'd Like to be a Teabag	Synonyms	Rhyming patterns
Check-up			

SKILLS		DEVELOPMENT	
Sentence		Text	Page
Verbs	Speech	Settings	4
Verb synonyms	Questions	Playscripts	10
Past tense	Speech marks	Settings	16
Compound nouns	Commas in lists	Poems on the same subject	22
Collective nouns	Ending sentences	Story beginnings	28
Adjectives	Commas	Story planning – plot and characters	34
Adjectives	Using commas with speech marks	Story planning – characters	40
Collective nouns	Using capital letters	Poetry – rhyming	46
Pronouns	Dialogue	First and third person	52
Gender words	Speech marks	How stories make you feel	58
Using 'was' and 'were'	Conjunctions	Book covers, blurbs and reviews	64
Pronouns and contractions	Order and time words	Humorous poetry	70
			76

A Home for Grandfather

William had problems. He missed his father, who had gone away from home. William also had to give up his bedroom because his grandfather was coming to live with them.

It was a wonderful room, and William loved it. It was big enough for him to be able to set out his model railway, and still have enough space to leave all his other toys lying about. William's habit of leaving his toys lying about was a problem, said his mother.

But William didn't think it was a problem – it was just handy.

The day came when Grandfather and his furniture would arrive . . . William went to school. . . . Then he went home and found a van standing outside the house. Grandfather's furniture had arrived.

William went to look at his old room. It was full of chests and a huge, old bed. The furniture almost filled the room.

"There will hardly be room for him to move about!" said William's mother.

"Why doesn't he get smaller furniture?" asked William.

"He's had these things a long time," said William's mother. "He's very fond of them. He doesn't want to give them up. It's a problem."

William went to look at his new room. It was very small and tidy – for there was no room to leave things lying about.

William liked to see his things lying about, and he understood how Grandfather felt about his old chests and his bed. But all the same he grumbled about his new little room all the way through tea.

From *William's Problems* by Shirley Isherwood

Comprehension

A Copy these sentences and fill in the missing words.

1 William could set out his ______ ______ in his room.

2 William had a habit of leaving his ______ lying about.

3 Grandfather's ______ almost filled the room.

4 William's new room was very ______ and ______ .

5 William understood how Grandfather felt about his ______ and his ______ .

B Think about the problems in the story.

1 What was the problem with Grandfather's furniture?

2 Why do you think this was a problem for William's Mum?

3 What problem did Grandfather's visit cause William?

4 Why do you think it was a problem for him?

C Write a sentence to answer each question.

1 How would you describe William's old room?

2 How would you describe William's new room?

3 Which room would you prefer? Why?

Vocabulary

Synonyms

Words that mean the same, or nearly the same, are called **synonyms.**
For example:
'big' and 'large' are synonyms
'tidy' and 'neat' are synonyms

A Find the pairs of synonyms in the box and write them in your book. The first one has been done to help you.

tiny small

tiny ✓	enough	under	maybe	untidy	break	shout	perhaps
obtain	small ✓	messy	get	sufficient	yell	smash	beneath

B Copy these sentences. Fill each gap with a synonym for the word in yellow.

1. It was a wonderful room and William loved it.
2. Grandfather was coming to live with them for a while.
3. William found a van waiting outside the house.
4. He understood how his grandfather felt.
5. William grumbled about his new little room.

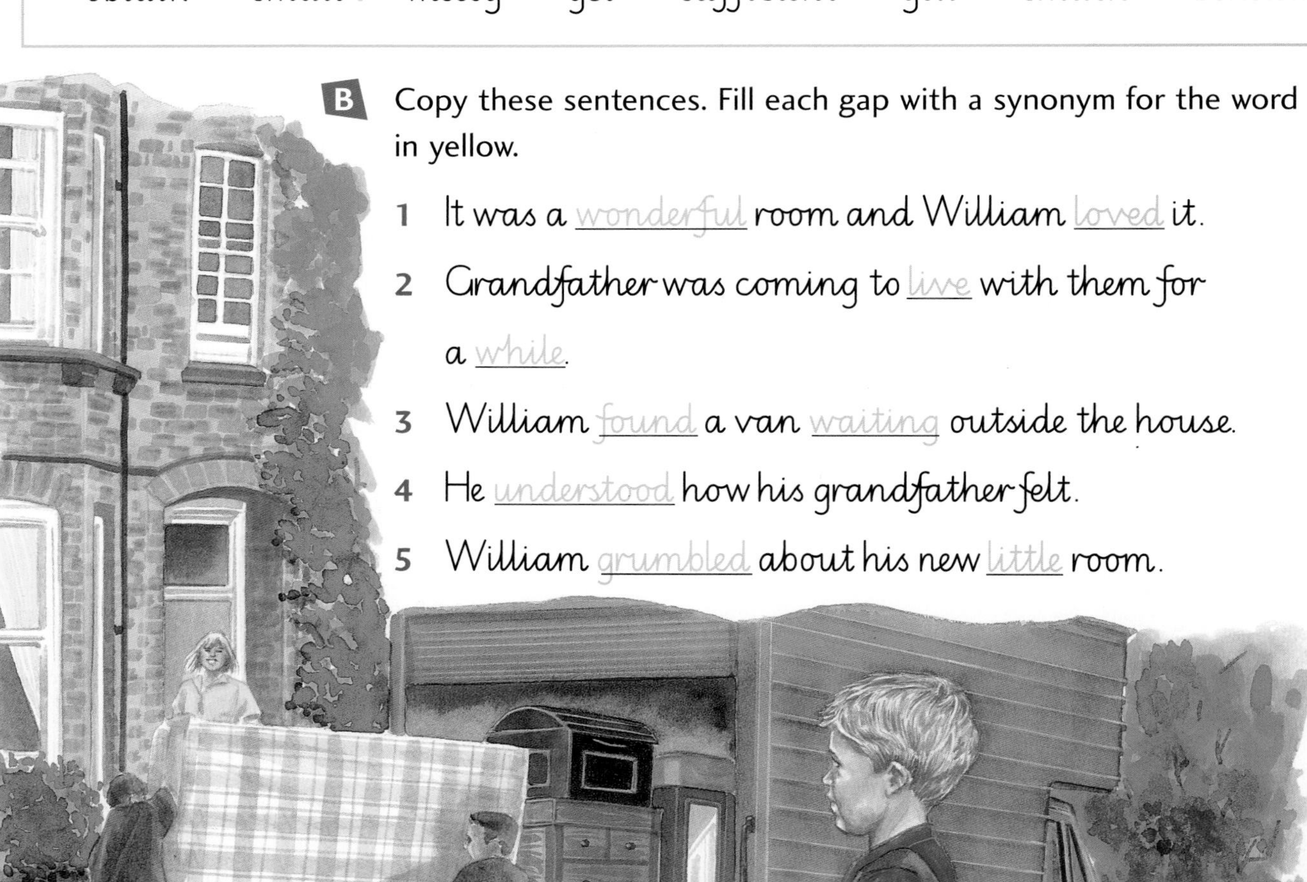

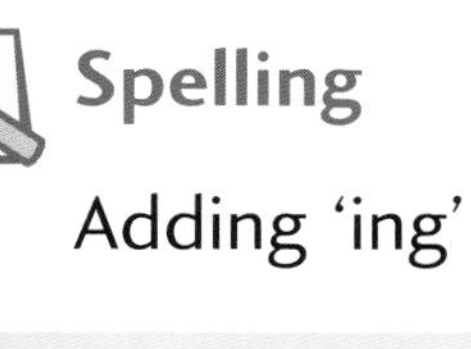

Spelling

Adding 'ing'

The letters a, e, i, o and u are **vowels**. All the rest are **consonants**.

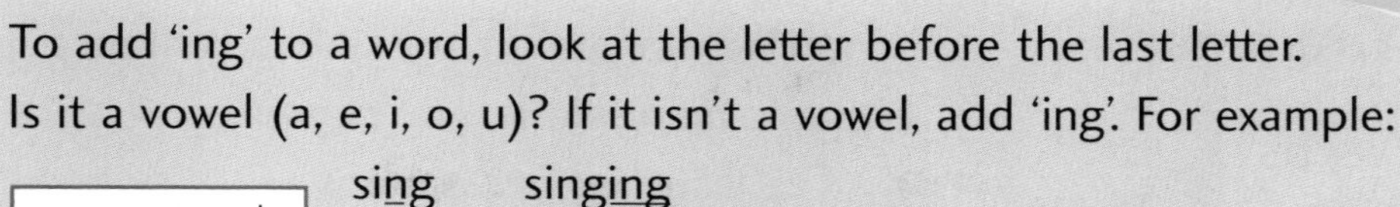

To add 'ing' to a word, look at the letter before the last letter.
Is it a vowel (a, e, i, o, u)? If it isn't a vowel, add 'ing'. For example:

consonant — sing singing

If it is a vowel, double the last letter, then add 'ing'. For example:

single vowel — hop hopping

But, if the letter before it is a vowel as well, just add 'ing'. For example:

two vowels — read reading

Be careful! This rule doesn't work for words ending in w, x or y.
For example:

play playing   draw drawing

A 1 Follow the rules to add 'ing' to each of these words.

a sit b run c stand d fall
e sleep f pay g cry h slip
i swim j eat k throw l fix

Usually, to add 'ing' to a word that ends with 'e', remove the 'e' and add 'ing'. For example:

come coming   live living

2 Add 'ing' to each of these words.

a skate b wave c make d dive
e stroke f mime g choke h live

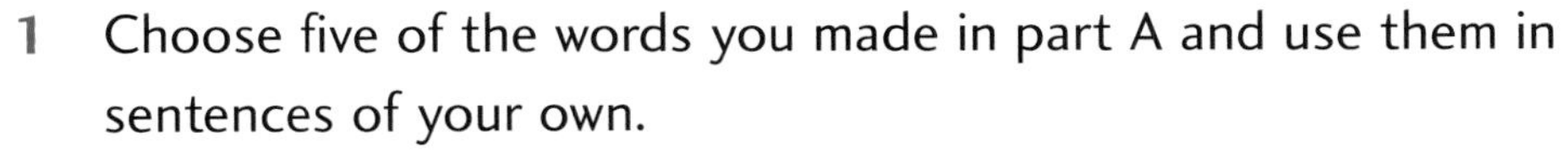

B 1 Choose five of the words you made in part A and use them in sentences of your own.

2 Write what each of these words was before 'ing' was added. The first one has been done to help you.

a driving drive b shaving c shaking
d having e hiding f liking g wiping

Grammar

Verbs

Verbs are sometimes called 'doing' words.

A **verb** is an 'action' word. In a sentence, a verb tells us what is being done. For example:

William went to school.
William loved his room.
He grumbled about his new room.

A Copy the two word webs below. Decide which web each verb from the box goes with and write it on the web. The first one has been done to help you.

skipping ✓	lifting	walking	pushing
running	shoving	heaving	dawdling

1 skipping ______ ______ ______ ______ (William going to school)

2 ______ ______ ______ ______ (moving Grandfather's furniture)

B Copy these sentences, adding a verb of your own to fill each gap.

1 William ______ his father.
2 His grandfather was ______ to live with them.
3 Mother said William must ______ into the small bedroom.
4 William left his things ______ on the floor.
5 Grandfather's furniture ______ the room.
6 William ______ about his new room.

Punctuation

Speech

In cartoons and drawings, what people say is sometimes shown in **speech bubbles**. For example:

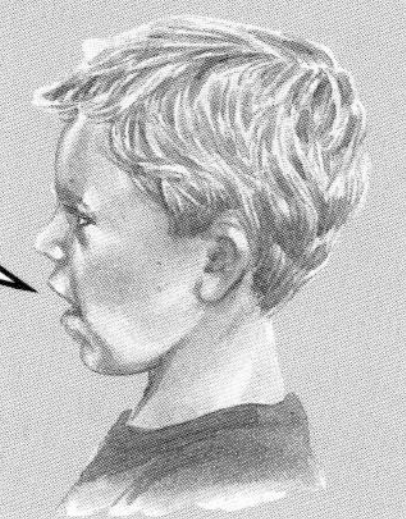

A Look at the box above.

1. Write the exact words William's mother spoke.
2. Write the exact words William spoke.

B

1. Draw some more pictures with speech bubbles to show what William and his mother said to each other next.
2. Look again at the story on page 4. Write the exact words William used when he asked Mum a question about Grandfather's furniture.

Writing

Settings

Where a story takes place is called the **setting**. You need to describe the setting of a story very carefully so the reader can imagine where events are happening.

A Think about the room where you sleep.

1. Make a list of the things in your room.
2. Think about the colours in your room. Make a list of the colours.
3. Write some sentences about your room. Begin your first sentence 'In my room I have …'

B Imagine you are going to write a story which takes place in a den you have made. The den is indoors because it is raining. Describe your den. Think about these questions:

- What did you use for the walls?
- What did you use for the roof?
- What did you use for the door?
- What does it feel like in your den?
- What is inside your den?

Hansel and Gretel

This is the beginning of the fairy story 'Hansel and Gretel'.

A woodcutter lived in a forest with his wife and their two young children. The woodcutter and his wife were very poor and did not have enough food to feed themselves and the children. One night, the woodcutter and his wife sat in front of their tiny fire and talked about what they could do.

"We had the last loaf of bread for our supper," said the woodcutter.

"I know," said his wife. "You didn't sell any wood today. What are we going to do?"

They looked around the bare cottage for something they could sell but there was nothing left. They decided that the only thing they could do was to leave the children in the forest and hope that some kind person would find them and look after them.

Comprehension

A Copy these sentences from the story and choose the correct words to finish them.

1 The woodcutter and his wife were homeless/poor/rich.

2 They did not have enough wood/children/food.

3 There was nothing left in the house to sell/burn/mend.

4 They decided to feed the children/leave the children in the forest/find someone to feed the children.

A play is a story that people watch being acted out, rather than read. When it is written down, a play looks different to a story.

Below is the beginning of the story of Hansel and Gretel, written as a playscript.

title

HANSEL AND GRETEL

scene setting

In the woodcutter's cottage.

characters

It is night and the children, HANSEL and GRETEL, are in bed.

WOODCUTTER: Come over to the fire, my dear, and sit down. We must talk.

WIFE: *(Sitting down)* Yes, we must talk.

dialogue

WOODCUTTER: We had the last loaf of bread for our supper.

WIFE: *(Crying)* I know. You didn't sell any wood today. What are we going to do?

WOODCUTTER: I don't know. *(Getting up and walking around the room)*

WIFE: Can we sell anything so that we can buy food?

WOODCUTTER: *(Looking around the room)* We have sold everything. There is nothing left.

WIFE: We must feed the children.

WOODCUTTER: *(Whispering)* We can't feed them. We must leave them in the forest and hope that some kind person will find them and look after them.

stage directions

Comprehension

B Write your answers to these questions about the playscript.

1 How many characters are there in this part of the play?

2 Where is the scene set?

3 Copy out one example of a stage direction.

4 Copy out one example of a piece of dialogue (spoken words).

C 1 What do you think of what the woodcutter and his wife are going to do?

2 How do you think the children will feel when they are left in the wood?

Vocabulary

Synonyms

Remember, **synonyms** are words or groups of words that mean the same, or nearly the same, e.g. 'extremely' is a synonym for 'very'.

A Write down pairs of words from the box that are synonyms.

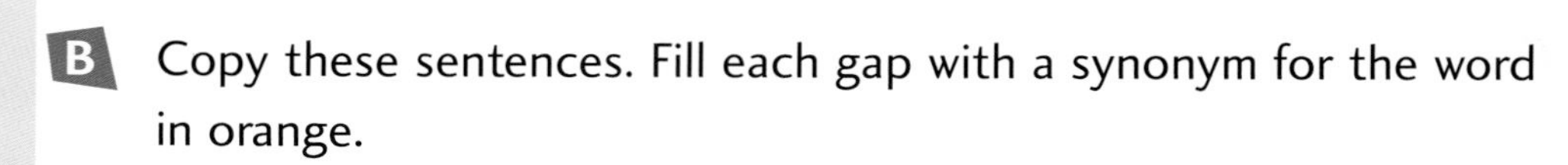

beginning searched find wealthy looked
forest rich discover wood start

B Copy these sentences. Fill each gap with a synonym for the word in orange.

1 Hansel and Gretel's parents were extremely poor.
2 There was not sufficient food for all of them.
3 The woodcutter and his wife discussed what they should do.
4 They decided to abandon the children in the forest.
5 Their mother was distraught at the thought of it.
6 The woodcutter said they had no alternative.

Spelling

Prefix 'un'

A **prefix** is a group of letters put at the beginning of a word to change its meaning. 'Un' is a very important prefix. Adding it changes a word to give it the opposite meaning. For example:

well <u>un</u>well
fair <u>un</u>fair

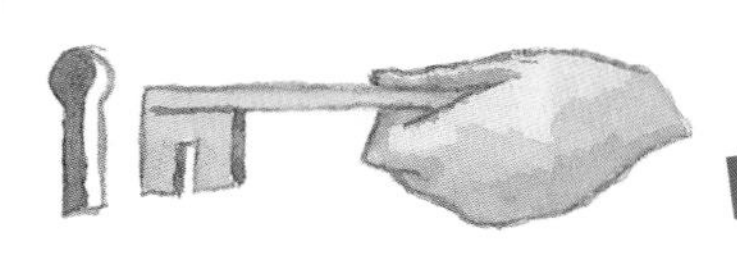

A Write the opposite of each word below.

1	lock	2	tidy	3	covered	4	hook
5	tie	6	safe	7	happy	8	roll
9	dress	10	wrap	11	do	12	true

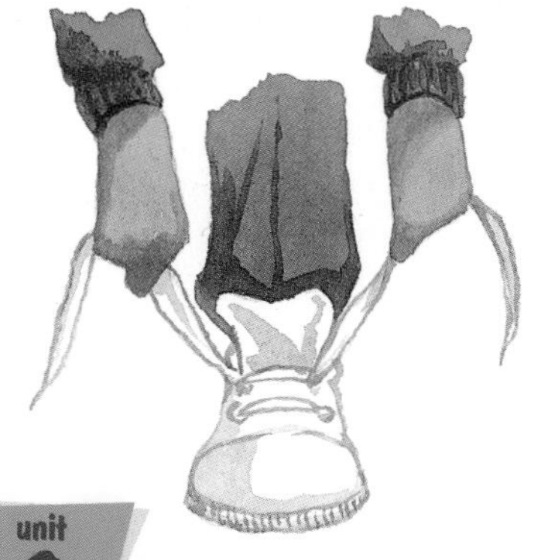

B Write a sentence that uses each of the following pairs of words. The first one has been done to help you.

1 kind unkind

It was unkind of the woodcutter to leave Hansel and Gretel in the wood, but he hoped some kind person would find them.

2 wrap unwrap
3 fold unfold
4 willing unwilling
5 able unable

Grammar

Verb synonyms

Here are some **verb synonyms**:

run chase sprint dash

They are all about moving quickly, but each has a slightly different meaning.

Remember, **verbs** are 'action' or 'doing' words.

A Draw a table like the one below. Write each verb from the box under the correct heading.

'look' words	'shout' words	'walk' words

look march hobble yell stroll shout
watch shriek gaze call stare walk

B Write two synonyms for each of the verbs below. The first one has been done to help you.

1 love like adore

2 hit 3 grab 4 join 5 push

Punctuation

Questions

A **?** at the end of a sentence shows it is a **question**. For example:
Can we sell anything so that we can buy food?

A Copy these sentences. Decide whether to put a question mark or a full stop at the end of each.

1 Will the children be safe in the forest __
2 Don't worry about them __
3 What will they have to eat __
4 Somebody will look after them __
5 When will we get some more money __

B Write a question to go with each of these answers. The first has been done to help you.

1 Their names were Hansel and Gretel.
What were the names of the two children?
2 Their father was a woodcutter.
3 They had a loaf of bread for supper.
4 There was nothing in the house they could sell.
5 The parents decided to leave the children in the forest.

Writing

Playscripts

When you write a **playscript**, you must include:

- where the scene is set – the setting;
- how many characters there are;
- the names of the characters;
- what each characters says – the dialogue;
- what each character does – the stage directions.

Below is part of a fairy story called 'Rumpelstiltskin'. The story took place in a country far away. A miller had a daughter. He was very proud of her, and told the King that she could spin gold out of straw. The King sent for the girl and took her to a room filled with piles of straw. He told her she had to turn all the straw into gold by the morning or she would be killed. The King left and locked the door behind him.

The girl began to weep.

"What shall I do?" she cried. "I can't turn straw into gold!"

Just then, the door opened and a strange little man hobbled in.

"What are you crying for?" he asked in a croaky voice.

"My father told the King I could spin straw into gold. The King wants all this straw turned into gold by the morning or I will die!"

"Can you spin the straw into gold?" asked the old man.

"No," replied the girl. "I don't know how."

"I do," said the old man. "What will you give me in return?"

"I'll give you my necklace," said the girl.

"That seems fair," agreed the old man, and he sat down and began to spin.

Write the extract from 'Rumpelstiltskin' as a playscript. Look carefully at page 11 to see how to set out your playscript. You do not need the orange lines but you could use different colours for the characters' names and the stage directions.

The Mice Who Lived in a Shoe

This is a story about a shoe . . . and the family of mice who lived in it. When it rained they got wet. When it snowed they got cold. When the sun shone, they got hot. When the wind blew, they flew all over the place. But the worst thing of all was when the cat put his paw into the shoe and stretched out his claws. The family huddled together at the toe end for safety. They all squeaked until the cat went away.

When they were sure the cat had gone, they gathered round Ma in the dark.

"The only way to be safe from the cat and to shelter from the weather," said Pa, "is to build a house."

"Where, where?" the family cried.

"Right here, in this shoe," replied Pa.

"What a good idea," said Ma, "I'll make the curtains."

"There'll be other things to do before that," observed Grandpa.

Pa asked everyone to draw their dream house. There was a big house, a small house, a short house, a tall house, a fat house, a thin house, a long house, a red house, a blue house and a green house.

Pa looked at them carefully to see who had the best ideas. Then he drew their dream house.

From *The Mice Who Lived in a Shoe* by Rodney Peppé

Comprehension

A

1. What were the types of weather that the shoe did not keep out?
2. What did the mice decide to do?
3. Make a list of the adjectives in the story which describe the different houses the mice drew.

B

1. What do you think Pa meant when he asked the mice to draw their 'dream house'?
2. Grandpa said they had 'other things' to do before they could put up curtains. Write down the things that you think the mice had to do to build their dream house.
3. What do you think turns a 'house' into a 'home'?

C The picture on the left shows the 'dream' house which the mice built. Write a description of it for someone who has not seen the picture.

Vocabulary

Synonyms – 'said'

"What a good idea," <u>said</u> Ma, "I'll make the curtains."
There are lots of **synonyms** for 'said'. For example:

replied   exclaimed   asked

Remember, the **synonym** of a word is a word that has a very similar meaning.

A Read through the passage from *The Mice Who Lived in a Shoe*, and write down the words that are synonyms of 'said'.

B Look at one or two story books that you have read. Make a list of other synonyms for 'said' that the writers use. There are lots!

Spelling

'i-e' and 'igh' letter patterns

The letter patterns 'i-e' and 'igh' often make the same sound.
For example:

m<u>i</u>c<u>e</u>   n<u>igh</u>t

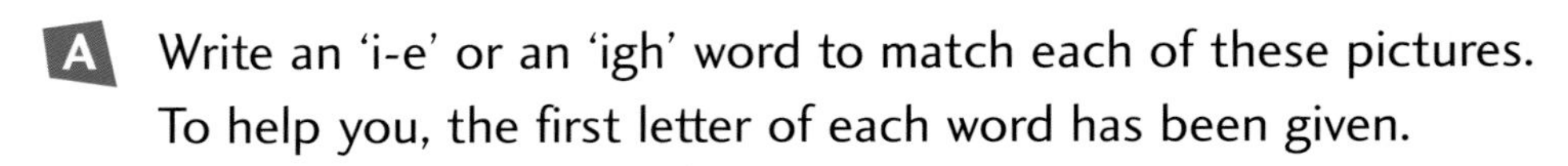

A Write an 'i-e' or an 'igh' word to match each of these pictures. To help you, the first letter of each word has been given.

1 b ______________

2 f ______________

3 f ______________

4 t ______________

5 p ______________

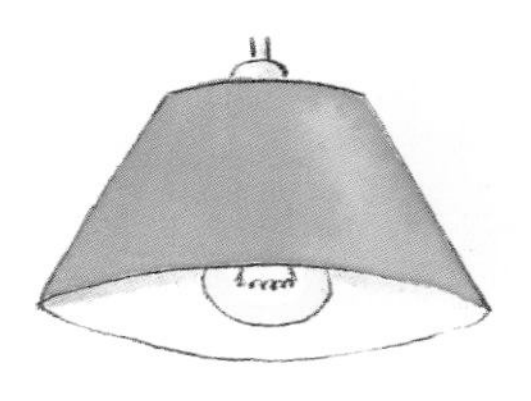

6 l ______________

B Write a word that rhymes with each word below and has the same spelling pattern. The first one has been done to help you.

1	file *pile*	2	sigh	3	bite	4	right
5	hide	6	mime	7	size	8	five
9	light	10	frighten	11	pride	12	line

Grammar

Past tense

'Live', 'living' and 'lived' are **verbs**.

When we write about something that is happening at the **present** time, we use the **present tense**. For example:

The mice live in the shoe.

or

The mice are living in the shoe.

When we write about something that has happened in the **past**, we use the **past tense**. For example:

The mice lived in the shoe.

The mice were living in the shoe.

A 1 The verbs below are in the present tense. Copy each one and write the past tense next to it. The first one has been done to help you.

a walk walked b jump c look

d ask e stretch f squeak

2 Write a sentence to say what you did to each word to change it from the present tense into the past tense.

B 1 The verbs below are in the present tense.
Copy each one and write the past tense next to it.

a fall b run c get

d draw e blow f sing

2 Write a sentence to say what you noticed about each verb when you changed it from the present tense into the past tense.

Punctuation

Speech marks

Speech marks are sometimes called **inverted commas**.

Sometimes we need to write down the exact words that someone has spoken. We use **speech marks** (“ ”) around the words that were said. For example:

“What a good idea,” said Ma.

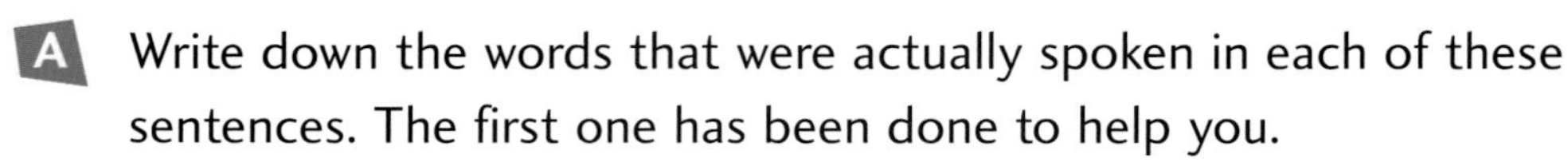

A Write down the words that were actually spoken in each of these sentences. The first one has been done to help you.

1. “The only way to be safe from the cat is to build a house,” said Pa.

   The only way to be safe from the cat is to build a house.
2. “Where, where?” the family cried.
3. “Right here in this shoe,” replied Pa.
4. “What a good idea. I'll make the curtains,” said Ma.
5. “There'll be other things to do before that,” observed Grandpa.
6. “I want you all to draw your dream house,” said Pa.

B Copy these sentences. Put speech marks around the words that the person actually spoke.

1. I don't like that cat, said Ma.
2. Neither do I, agreed Pa.
3. I worry that the cat will harm us, said Ma anxiously.
4. A house would keep us warm and dry as well, added Pa.
5. I agree, said Grandpa.

Writing

Remember, the **setting** of a story is where it takes place.

Settings

A 1 The setting for the opening of *The Mice Who Lived in a Shoe* is an old shoe. Think about a story you could write that takes place in your home. Choose the room where your story begins and describe the room carefully. You could also draw a picture.

2 Imagine you are going to write a story set in your school. Write a description of your classroom or another room in the school where your story might start.

Dialogue

B 1 Look at page 16. Write down:

a something that Pa said
b something that Ma said
c something that Grandpa said.

2 Imagine you were one of the mice that lived in the shoe with Pa, Ma and Grandpa. Write down what you would have said when Pa decided to build a house. Remember to put the spoken words in speech marks.

Winter Morning

Winter is the king of showmen,
Turning tree stumps into snowmen
And houses into birthday cakes
And spreading sugar over lakes.
Smooth and clean and frosty white,
The world looks good enough to bite.
That's the season to be young,
Catching snowflakes on your tongue.
Snow is snowy when it's snowing,
I'm sorry it's slushy when it's going.

by Ogden Nash

Snow

It's snowing today.
It was snowing yesterday
and the day before.
The planes can't fly,
the trains are stuck
and the road's a big ice lolly
that I can't suck.
The postman's van
is stuck up the road
and the milkman's slipping
with his clinky load.
The snow has blown
against our door
and the radio says
there'll be lots more
because it's snowing today.
It was snowing yesterday
and the day before.

by Ian McMillan and Martyn Wiley

Comprehension

A Write a sentence to answer each question.

These questions are about 'Winter Morning':

1. What does the snow make the tree stumps look like?
2. What does the snow make the houses look like?
3. Find three words in the poem which describe the snow.
4. What does the snow look like when it is 'going'?

These questions are about 'Snow':

5. How long has it been snowing?
6. What two things in the poem are 'stuck'?
7. How do we know it is windy?
8. How do we know it is going to keep on snowing?

B In 'Winter Morning':

1. Why do you think the poet says the tree stumps look like snowmen?
2. Why do you think the poet says the houses look like birthday cakes?

In 'Snow':

3. Why do you think the poet says that 'the road's a big ice lolly'?
4. Why does the milkman have a 'clinky load'?

C The poets feel differently about the snow.

Look at 'Winter Morning'.

1. How do you think the poet feels about snow?
2. How does the poem make you feel?

Look at 'Snow'.

3. How do you think the poets feel about snow?
4. How does the poem make you feel?

Vocabulary

Using a dictionary

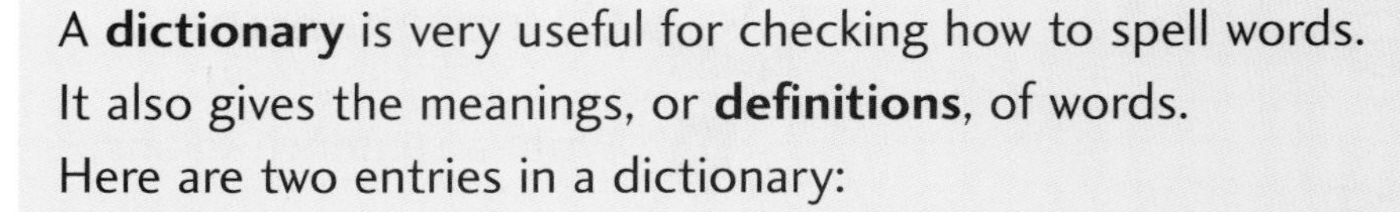

A **dictionary** is very useful for checking how to spell words.
It also gives the meanings, or **definitions**, of words.
Here are two entries in a dictionary:

noun — definition

tongue *n* the fleshy organ in the mouth for licking and tasting.
toss *v* to throw into the air.

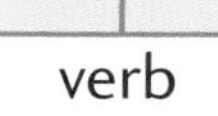

verb — definition

A Write the answers to these questions.

1. Is 'toss' a noun or a verb?
2. Is 'tongue' a noun or a verb?
3. What is a tongue?
4. What does 'toss' mean?

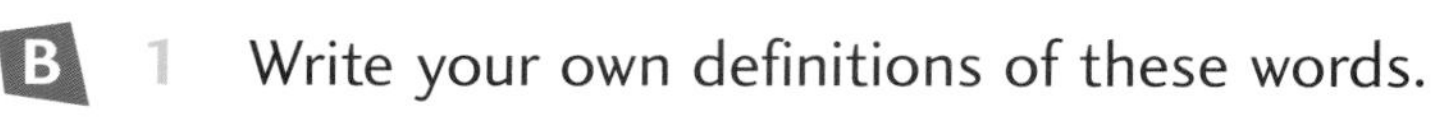

B 1 Write your own definitions of these words.

a winter   b snow   c blizzard   d trudge

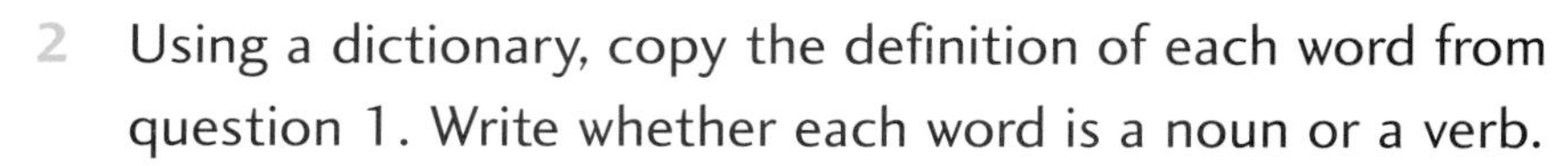

2 Using a dictionary, copy the definition of each word from question 1. Write whether each word is a noun or a verb.

Spelling

'ow' letter pattern

The 'ow' letter pattern can make two different sounds. For example:

The cl<u>ow</u>n played in the sn<u>ow</u>.

A How many 'ow' words can you see in this picture?

B Write each word from the box under the correct heading. Two have been done to help you.

how ✓	own ✓	crown	bowl	down	
know	flower	flow	howl	blow	
now	low	owl	tow	towel	town
gown	frown	slow	brown	show	

'ow' words like 'clown'	'ow' words like 'snow'
how	own

Grammar

Compound nouns

Remember, a noun is the name of a thing, for example:

snow  man 

egg cup

Sometimes we join two small words together to make one **compound noun**, for example:

snow + man = snowman  egg + cup = eggcup 

A Join each pair of words to make a compound noun. Then write a sentence using your new word.

1 house farm 2 birth day

3 snow flake 4 pot tea

B The words in the box can be joined up in different ways to make eleven different compound nouns. Write down at least eight.

step	ball	rain	drift	print	door
snow	drop	storm	flake	foot	

Punctuation

Commas in lists

We use a **comma** (,) to separate each word in a list. For example:

Yesterday we had fog, frost, wind, rain and snow.

Notice that, instead of a comma, we put 'and' between the last two items in the list.

A Copy these sentences and add the missing commas.

1. The snow fell on the trees houses lakes and children.
2. Snow is a problem for aeroplanes trains vans buses and cars.
3. Last week it snowed on Monday Tuesday Thursday Friday and Saturday.

B Answer each question with a sentence that contains a list.

1. What presents would you most like for Christmas?
2. What might you wear on a really cold day?
3. What four things do you most enjoy doing when it snows?
4. Which of your friends enjoy the snow?

Writing

Poems on the same subject

The two poems, 'Winter Morning' and 'Snow', are about the **same subject**, but the poets have different views.

'Winter Morning' tells us all the good things about snow.
'Snow' tells us all the bad things about snow.

A Think about rain.

1. Write a list of words and phrases you could use if you were writing a poem to show that you don't like rain.
2. Write a list of words and phrases you could use if you were writing a poem to show that you like rain.

B Choose one of these animals:

- cat 
- dog 
- spider 

Decide whether you like this type of animal or not.
Write a short poem, describing the animal, so your reader can guess if you like it or don't like it.

A poem doesn't have to rhyme.

Animal Tales

The Hippo and the Elephant

Here is the beginning of a story about how a little mouse stopped the hippopotamus and the elephant from arguing.

Now, the hippo and elephant were forever squabbling over who was the stronger. The other animals were getting really fed up with them until, one day, the little mouse had an idea.

First, Mouse went to find Hippo, who was asleep in the water hole.

"You might think that you are strong, but you're not as strong as me. I bet I could get you out of that water hole," said Mouse.

"Ho! Ho! Ho! Don't make me laugh! I'm the strongest animal in the whole world," grunted the sleepy Hippo, and closed his eyes for a quiet doze in the cool pool. "There is no way you could pull me out of the water!"

Next, Mouse went to find Elephant, who was asleep in the shade of some bushes near the water hole.

"You might think that you are strong, but you're not as strong as me. I bet I could get you into that water hole," said Mouse.

"Ho! Ho! Ho! Don't make me laugh! I'm the strongest animal in the whole world," grunted the sleepy Elephant, and closed his eyes for a quiet doze in the shade of the bushes. "There is no way you could pull me into the water."

Mouse went away and came scurrying back with a huge coil of rope …

Comprehension

A Copy these sentences and fill in the missing words.

1. Hippo and Elephant were always ______ .
2. The other ______ were getting really fed up with them.
3. "There is no way you could pull me out of the ______!" said Hippo.
4. Elephant was asleep in the ______ of some bushes.
5. Mouse went to fetch a huge ______ of rope.

How the Crab got the Crack in its Back

This traditional folk tale from Trinidad has been told by parents to their children, and by those children to their children, and so on for many, many years.

Once upon a time, there were just two crabs in the world. One day, one of the crabs went to the river to bathe and saw an old woman sitting on a log.

"Scratch my back," said the old woman. She did not say 'please' and she did not smile. In fact, she was rather ugly, but the crab was kind-hearted and did as the old woman asked. This pleased the old woman very much. She then asked the crab to take a big shell and fill it with cool water for her to drink. The kind crab did so, and the woman was refreshed.

Now, this old woman was a fairy, which you have probably already guessed. She said to the kind crab, "You are a good, kind crab so I will do something for you now." She sprinkled a few drops of water on the crab, who instantly turned into a beautiful bird with brightly coloured feathers.

The crab rushed off to tell the other crab what had happened. The other crab wanted to be turned into a beautiful bird as well, so she went down to the river to see the old woman …

Comprehension

Write down your answers to these questions.

B

1. Find two words in the story that describe the woman.
2. Why did the crab do as the woman asked?
3. Why did the woman want to do something for the crab?
4. What did the woman do for the crab?
5. What did the crab do next?

C

1. How do you think the story of *The Hippo and the Elephant* ends? Think about what Mouse might do with the huge coil of rope.
2. How do you think the story 'How the Crab got the Crack in its Back' ends? Think about how the second crab might treat the old woman.
3. Which of the two story openings would make you want to go on reading? Why?

Vocabulary

Letter order

1 Here is a message, written in code. Be a detective! Use the code-breaker to work out what the message says. The first word has been done to help you.

20 8 5   12 9 20 20 12 5   13 15 21 19 5
T H E

23 1 19   20 8 5   3 12 5 22 5 18 5 19 20

1 14 9 13 1 12

Code-breaker:

A	B	C	D	E	F	G	H	I	J	K	L	M	N	O	P	Q	R	S	T	U	V	W	X	Y	Z
1	2	3	4	5	6	7	8	9	10	11	12	13	14	15	16	17	18	19	20	21	22	23	24	25	26

2 Write the following letters in alphabetical order.

H C X R A P K D Z S

B

1 Write this sentence in code:

The crabs saw an old woman sitting on a log.

2 Write words or letters to answer these questions.

a Which two letters are closest to the centre of the alphabet?

b A is the first vowel in the alphabet. Where do the other vowels come?

c Which letter comes nearest to the middle of the first half of the alphabet?

d Which letter comes nearest to the middle of the second half of the alphabet?

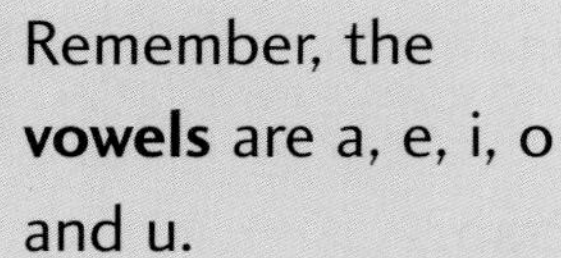

Remember, the **vowels** are a, e, i, o and u.

Spelling

Comparing words

A thing can be bigger or smaller than **one** other thing.
A thing can be the biggest or smallest of **three or more** things.

For example:

The mouse is **smaller** than an elephant.
The mouse is the **smallest** animal in the story.

A Copy the sentences below. Choose a word from the box to complete each sentence.

strongest
bigger
biggest
smaller

1 The elephant is ______ than the mouse.
2 The mouse is ______ than the hippo.
3 The elephant is the ______ of all the animals.
4 Hippo said he was the ______ animal in the world.

If a comparing word ends with 'y', we change the 'y' to 'i' before adding 'er' or 'est', for example:

happy happier happiest

B Write each of these adjectives with an 'er' ending and then with an 'est' ending.

1 pretty 2 silly 3 busy 4 merry

Grammar

Collective nouns

A **noun** is the name of a person, place or thing.
A **collective noun** is a special name for a group (collection) of people, places or things. For example:

a herd of elephants

A Match each noun from Box A with the correct collective noun from Box B. Write down the pairs of words.

A	B
elephants books	team crowd
people sheep players	herd crew library
sailors trees	forest flock

B 1 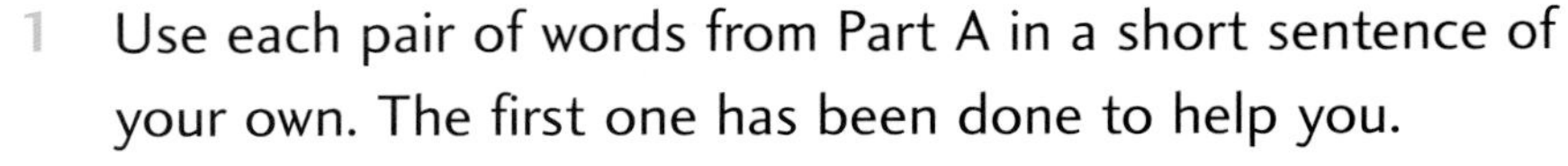
Use each pair of words from Part A in a short sentence of your own. The first one has been done to help you.

The flock of sheep was on the hill.

2 Below are some collective nouns for groups of people. What would you expect each group of people to be doing?

a an orchestra
b an audience
c a congregation
d a choir
e a queue
f a crowd

Use a dictionary if you need help.

Punctuation

Ending sentences

Remember, we use a **full stop** (.) to end most sentences, but we use a **question mark** (?) when the sentence is a question. When the sentence is an exclamation (something unusual, surprising or exciting), we use an **exclamation mark** (!).

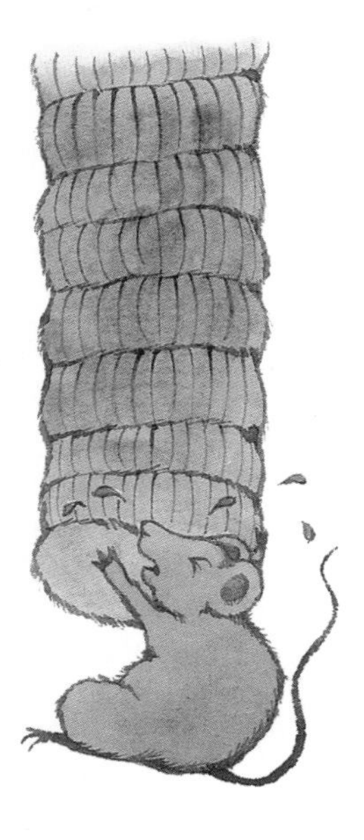

A Copy these sentences and add the missing punctuation marks.

1 Is an elephant bigger than a hippopotamus _
2 What is the mouse going to do with the rope _
3 The old woman wanted a drink of water _
4 "Help _" screamed the crab.

B Write six sentences about *How the Crab got the Crack in its Back.* Write two that finish with an exclamation mark, two that finish with a question mark and two that finish with a full stop.

Writing

Story beginnings

The **beginning** of a story must make the reader want to go on reading. You can begin a story:

- by describing the setting;
- by telling your reader about the characters;
- with a conversation.

This is the beginning of a story called *The Weirdstone of Brisingamen* by Alan Garner:

The guard knocked on the door of the compartment as he went past. "Wilmslow, fifteen minutes!"

"Thank you!" shouted Colin.

Susan began to clear away the debris of the journey – apple cores, orange peel, food wrappings, magazines, while Colin pulled down their luggage from the rack.

GLOSSARY
debris rubbish

A **glossary** in a book explains what some of the words mean.

The beginning of the story tells us that:

- Colin and Susan are on a train;
- they are going to Wilmslow;
- the train will arrive in fifteen minutes.

It makes us want to find out:

- who Colin and Susan are;
- why they are going to Wilmslow;
- who will be waiting for them.

A Read the story beginnings below.

1 Write about what the beginning of each story tells you.
2 What does each one make you want to find out?

When Mary Lennox was sent to Mistlethwaite Manor to live with her uncle, everybody said she was the most disagreeable-looking child ever seen.

From *The Secret Garden* by Frances Hodgson Burnett

"Your Auntie Betty has copped it," said Pa Hedgehog to Ma.
"Oh, no!" cried Ma. "Where?"
"Just down the road. Opposite the newsagent's. Bad place to cross, that."
"Everywhere's a bad place to cross nowadays," said Ma.
"The traffic's dreadful."

From *The Hodgeheg* by Dick King-Smith

GLOSSARY
copped it been killed

B Write the beginning of your own story in which an animal is kind to an old lady who is really a fairy.

- You could describe the setting of your story.
- You could tell the reader about your characters.
- You could begin with a conversation.

Merlin

Merlin was a wise old wizard who lived long ago. He was able to see what was going to happen in the future. He could also work magic spells.

King Uther had a baby son called Arthur. All the knights wanted to be king when Uther died. Merlin knew they would try to kill Arthur. Merlin took the baby away and gave him to an old friend to look after.

When King Uther died, the knights fought each other to see who should be king. No one but Merlin knew Uther had a son.

Merlin knew that Arthur should be king. All the knights were invited to try to pull a sword out of a big stone. The one who could do it would be king.

None of the knights could pull the sword out of the stone.

Arthur stepped forward and, to everyone's surprise, pulled the sword from the stone and was crowned king.

Comprehension

GLOSSARY
knights men who dressed in armour and fought on horseback

A Write a sentence to answer each question.

1. What two unusual things could Merlin do?
2. Why did Merlin take baby Arthur away?
3. Why did the knights try to pull the sword out of the stone?
4. Who pulled the sword out of the stone?
5. What happened next?

B Make a list of:

1. the characters in the story;
2. the things that happen in the story.

C Draw a poster, inviting the knights to try to pull the sword out of the stone. Use pictures and words on your poster to show:

- what has to be done with the sword;
- who is invited to try;
- what will happen to the person who pulls the sword out of the stone.

Vocabulary

Antonyms

Antonyms are words that have opposite meanings. For example:
'thick' and 'thin' are antonyms
'wet' and 'dry' are antonyms

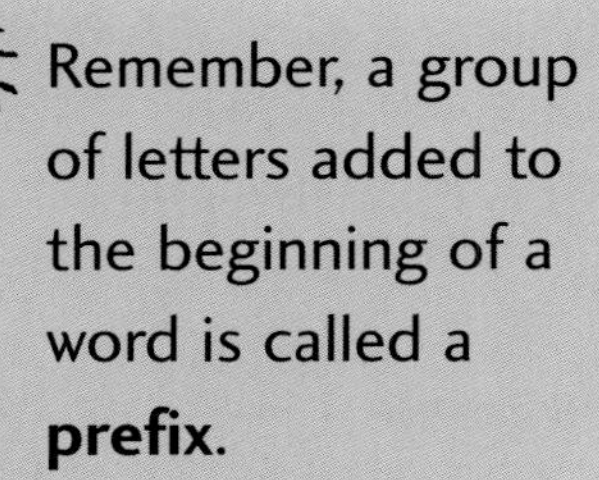

A 1 Choose from the box the antonym of each word.

a sad	ill happy frightened silly
b large	dirty full big small
c rough	cold smooth heavy hard
d pull	lift push throw carry
e future	ahead past present behind

2 Choose three pairs of antonyms from question 1. Write a sentence using each pair. For example:
The wide bed wouldn't fit through the narrow door.

Remember, a group of letters added to the beginning of a word is called a **prefix**.

Adding the **prefix** 'un' or 'dis' to a word can sometimes make the **antonym**, for example:

happy	unhappy
pleased	displeased

B 1 Use 'un' or 'dis' to make the antonym of each word.

a pack b like c attractive d agree
e well f certain g trust h true

2 Write a sentence to explain what happened to the meaning of the words in question 1 when 'un' or 'dis' was added.

3 Choose three pairs of antonyms from question 1. Use them in sentences of your own.

Spelling

Silent letters

Words that sound the same but have different spellings and different meanings are called **homophones**, for example:

'knight' and 'night' — The knight rode through the dark night.
'hour' and 'our' — Our train leaves in an hour.

We do not say the 'k' in 'knight' and the 'h' in 'hour'. They are called **silent letters**.

A Use each pair of homophones in a short sentence of your own.

1 knot not 2 know no 3 knew new

B 1 Copy these words into your book. Draw a circle around the silent letter in each word.

a knife b lamb c knee d write
e comb f wrap g sword h answer
i whistle j honest k hour l hymn

2 Write down five more words that have a silent letter.
Hint: Try thinking of words that begin with the silent letters 'k', 'w' and 'h'.

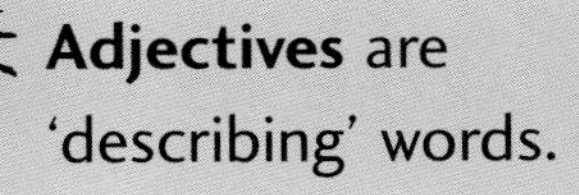

Grammar

Adjectives

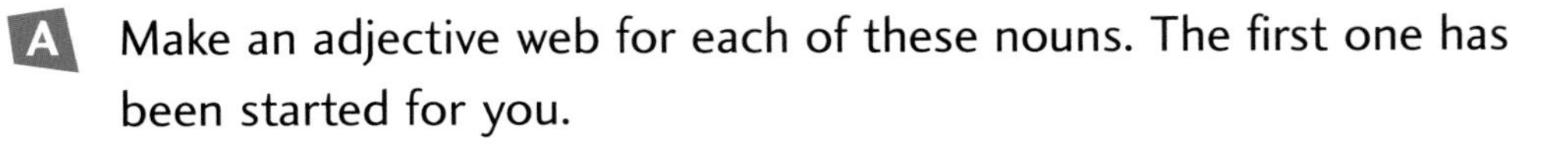

Remember, **adjectives** tell us more about nouns. For example:

Merlin was a wise wizard.

The adjective 'wise' tells us about the wizard.

Adjectives are 'describing' words.

A Make an adjective web for each of these nouns. The first one has been started for you.

trusted brave

1 knight

2 spells
3 sword
4 stone

B Copy these sentences. Replace each underlined adjective with an interesting one of your own. The first one has been done for you.

1. The <u>old</u> knight rode on his <u>big</u> horse.
   The <u>brave</u> knight rode on his <u>white</u> horse.
2. Merlin took the <u>little</u> baby away to his <u>secret</u> cave.
3. The <u>ill</u> King wanted Arthur to be King after he died.
4. Merlin the wizard had a <u>good</u> plan.

Punctuation

Commas

If 'yes' or 'no' is at the beginning of a sentence, we put a **comma** after it. For example:

Yes, Merlin was happy to look after the baby.

Commas are also used in sentences to show the reader when to pause. For example:

When Uther died, the knights fought each other.

A Rewrite these sentences, putting in the commas.

1. Arthur stepped up took a deep breath and pulled hard on the sword.
2. No Merlin was not a wicked wizard.
3. Yes Merlin wanted Arthur to be King.

Remember, commas are also used in lists, in place of 'and'. For example:

Tom, Ben, Leah and Kate went bowling.

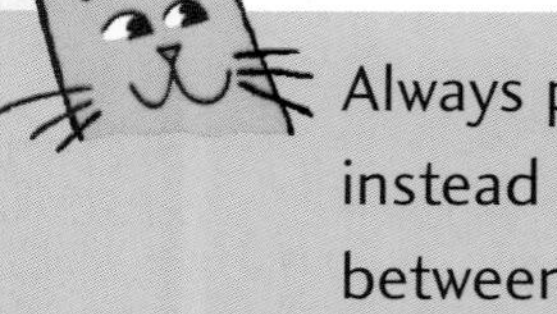

Always put 'and' instead of a comma between the last two items in a list.

B Rewrite these sentences using commas correctly. Leave out 'and' when possible.

1. The knights liked riding and jousting and feasting.
2. A knight's strong armour covered his head and body and arms and hands and legs and feet.

Writing

Story planning – plot

Before you begin to write a story, you need to plan what is going to happen. You need to plan:

- how your story begins;
- what happens in the middle of your story;
- how you are going to end your story.

A short description of what happens in a story is called the **plot**. A plot has facts but no details.

The plot of Merlin's story is on pages 34–35.

A 1 Write the plot of this story by saying what is happening in each picture.

2 Write the plot of a story called 'The Magic Hat'.

- How does your story begin?
- What happens in the middle of your story?
- How does your story end?

Story planning – characters

You have to think carefully about the characters in your stories. You need to know:

- what they look like;
- what sort of people they are.

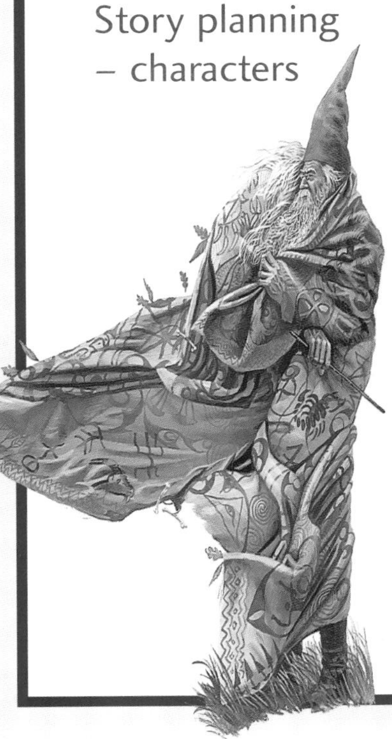

B Look at this picture of Merlin the magician.

Imagine you are describing Merlin to a friend who has not seen this picture. Look carefully at the picture and write a description of Merlin.

- What is he wearing?
- What pictures are on his clothes?
- What does his hat look like?
- What is he carrying?
- What sort of person do you think Merlin is?

Theseus and the Minotaur

Below is part of an old Greek myth about one of the adventures of Theseus, a Greek hero. Theseus's father, Aegeus, was King of Athens. Minos, the King of Crete, was going to attack Athens unless Aegeus sent seven women and seven men to Crete. They were to be fed to the Minotaur, a monster who was half man, half beast and who lived in the middle of a maze.

King Aegeus told Theseus about the Minotaur.

"I will go, myself, and meet this Minotaur," said Theseus.

His father begged him not to be so foolish, but Theseus wouldn't listen. He was young, brave and strong and he was sure he could kill the Minotaur.

"I will kill the Minotaur and then no more men and women will have to die," he said.

When Theseus and the other young people arrived in Crete, King Minos was friendly. They were treated very well and given games to play and rich food to eat. Princess Ariadne, King Minos's beautiful young daughter, saw Theseus and immediately fell in love with him.

Ariadne did not want Theseus to be fed to the horrible Minotaur. "You must ask to be the first one to go into the maze tomorrow," she whispered. "Here is a ball of string. Fasten one end to the door when they have locked you in. Unroll the string as you go through the maze and it will help you to find your way back. I will be at the door at midnight to let you out."

The next day, Theseus did as the Princess said. He unrolled the string as he searched for the middle of the maze. When he found it, the Minotaur was waiting for him. The Minotaur was horrible! It had a huge human body and the neck and head of a bull. When the Minotaur saw Theseus, it rushed at him bellowing loudly.

Theseus was not afraid. He jumped to one side and punched the Minotaur over the heart. Every time the Minotaur rushed at him, Theseus punched it again. At last, the Minotaur began to grow weak. Theseus jumped onto its back, took hold of the great horns and forced its head back. There was a mighty crack as the Minotaur's neck broke!

Theseus picked up the end of the string and began to find his way back . . .

Comprehension

A Write 'true' or 'false' for each of these sentences.

1. The Minotaur was the King of Crete.
2. Princess Ariadne was King Minos's daughter.
3. Princess Ariadne gave Theseus a ball to play with.
4. The Minotaur lived in the middle of a maze.
5. The Minotaur had the head of a bull.

B

1. Make a list of the characters in the story.
2. Make a list of the events in the story.

C Write words and phrases to answer these questions.

1. How do you think King Aegeus felt when Theseus said he would go to meet the Minotaur?
2. What do you think of Ariadne's plan?
3. How do you think King Minos would feel if he knew what his daughter had done?

Vocabulary

Using a dictionary

Remember, a **dictionary** is useful for checking spelling and meaning.

immediate *adj* needing to be done now, immediately, at once
immense *adj* huge, gigantic
immerse *v* to plunge into water
imp *n* a small devil
important *adj* of great interest
impossible *adj* not possible
imprison *v* to put in prison

A On the left is part of a page from a dictionary. Use the information to decide which is the correct spelling of each word. Write the answers in your book.

1 immedaitely immediately immediatly imediately

2 imposible impossable impossible impossibal

3 inprison imprision inprisin imprison

4 inportant impotant importent important

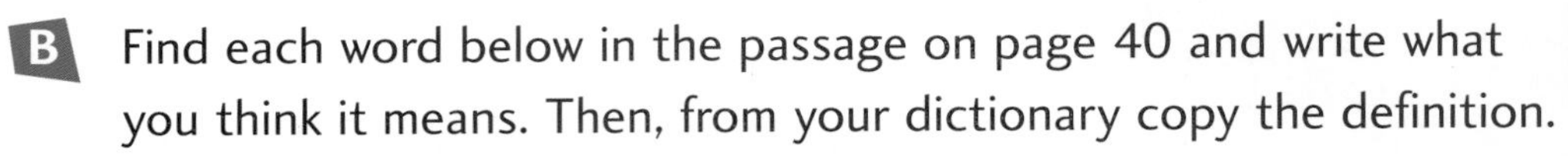

B Find each word below in the passage on page 40 and write what you think it means. Then, from your dictionary copy the definition.

1 myth   2 adventure   3 horrible   4 maze

Spelling

Contractions

Remember, a **contraction** is used in place of two words. For example:

Theseus <u>wouldn't</u> listen.

wouldn't is a contraction of 'would not'

Here are some more contractions:

he will = he'll   do not = don't   you are = you're

Contractions are made by leaving out some letters and putting an apostrophe (') in their place.

A Write each of these contractions as two words.

1 she'll 2 they're 3 shouldn't 4 can't 5 we'd

B 1 Write the contraction for each pair of words.

a they will b could not c they have d is not

2 Copy these sentences, replacing the words in blue with contractions.

a <u>Here is</u> a ball of string.

b Unroll the string as <u>you are</u> going along.

c <u>You will</u> need it to find your way back.

Grammar

Adjectives

Remember, **adjectives** tell us more about nouns.
They can tell us about people's moods and feeling. For example:

She was an <u>unhappy</u> princess.

A Find the adjective in each sentence and write it down.

1. Theseus was a brave Greek.
2. His father said he was a foolish young man.
3. The Minotaur was a horrible monster.
4. Ariadne became a happy princess when Theseus returned.

Sometimes other words can be used with adjectives to add more detail. For example:

Ariadne became an <u>**extremely**</u> **happy** princess.

B Add an adjective to each word from the box. Use each pair of words in a sentence about the picture. The first one has been done to help you.

The Minotaur was the <u>most ugly</u> creature he had ever seen.

most ✓ very extremely quite slightly

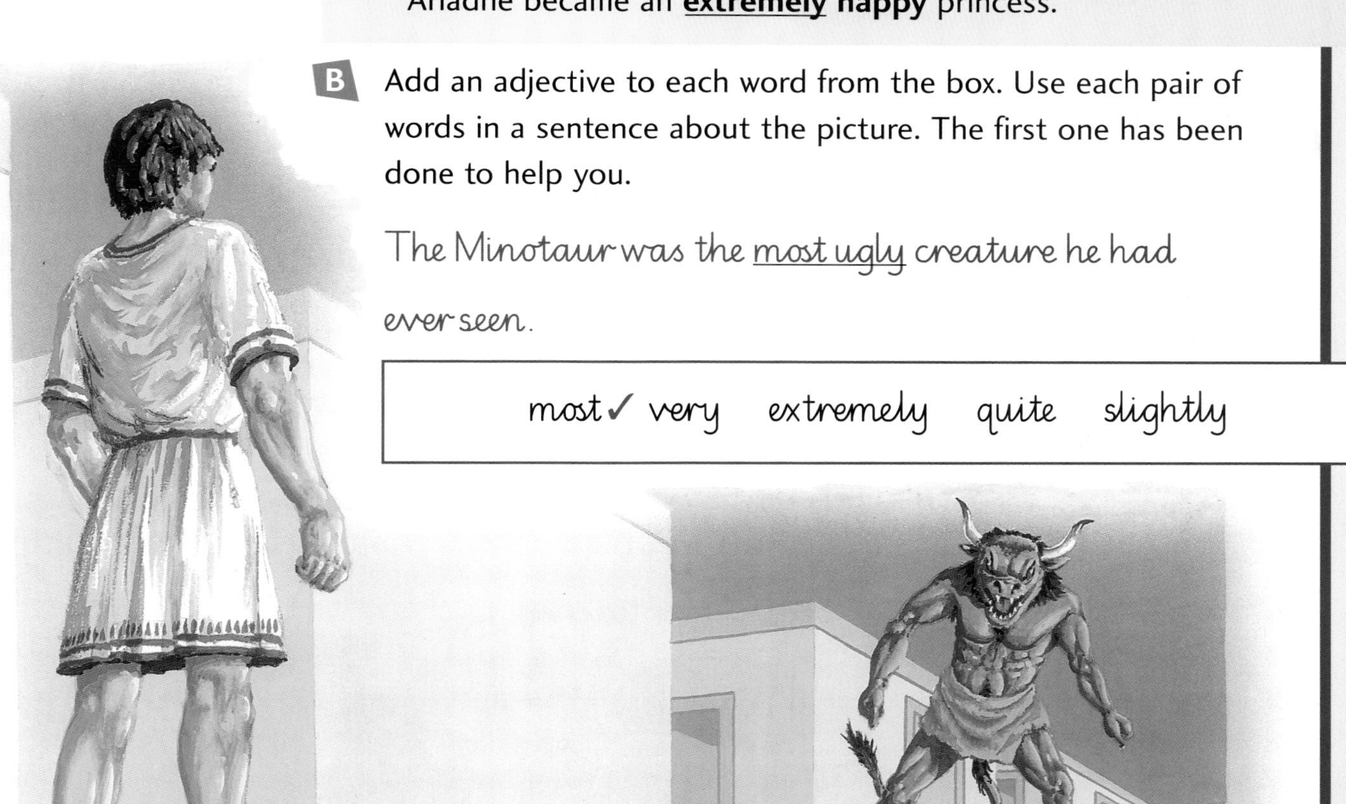

Punctuation

Using commas with speech marks

Remember, we use **speech marks** (“ ”) around the words that somebody actually said.

If there is more text after the end of the speech marks, we put a comma at the end of the words spoken, inside the speech marks. For example:

“I’m afraid they will attack us,” said the King.

A Copy these sentences, adding the missing commas.

1 “Please come home safely ” cried the old King.
2 “I will be careful ” said Theseus.
3 “You are the bravest person I’ve ever met ”said the Princess.
4 “I have a plan to save you ” whispered the Princess.
5 “I will kill the monster ” said Theseus boldly.

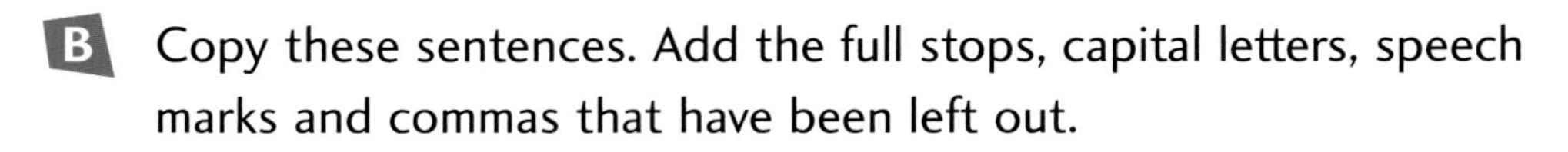

B Copy these sentences. Add the full stops, capital letters, speech marks and commas that have been left out.

1 i shall read you a story said their teacher
2 mrs fry always chooses good stories whispered sundeep
3 yes i like listening to stories agreed sam
4 please sit quietly on the carpet said mrs fry
5 today i will read a story from my book of greek myths began their teacher

Writing

Story planning – characters

The people or animals in a story are called the **characters**.
The characters in 'Theseus and the Minotaur' are:

King Aegeus
Theseus
King Minos
Princess Ariadne
The Minotaur

Sometimes, a writer describes what a character looks like and what sort of person they are. What a character says and does also helps us to decide what they are like.

A Copy and complete the table. The first part has been done to help you.

Character	What they look like	What sort of person they are
King Aegeus	old	loves his son quite weak
Theseus		
King Minos		
Princess Ariadne		
The Minotaur		

B After killing the Minotaur, Theseus gets out of the maze and sails for home.

Think about an adventure he could have on his way home.

Think of three new characters who could be in his adventure. Make up names for the characters. Describe what they look like. Write about what sort of characters they are.

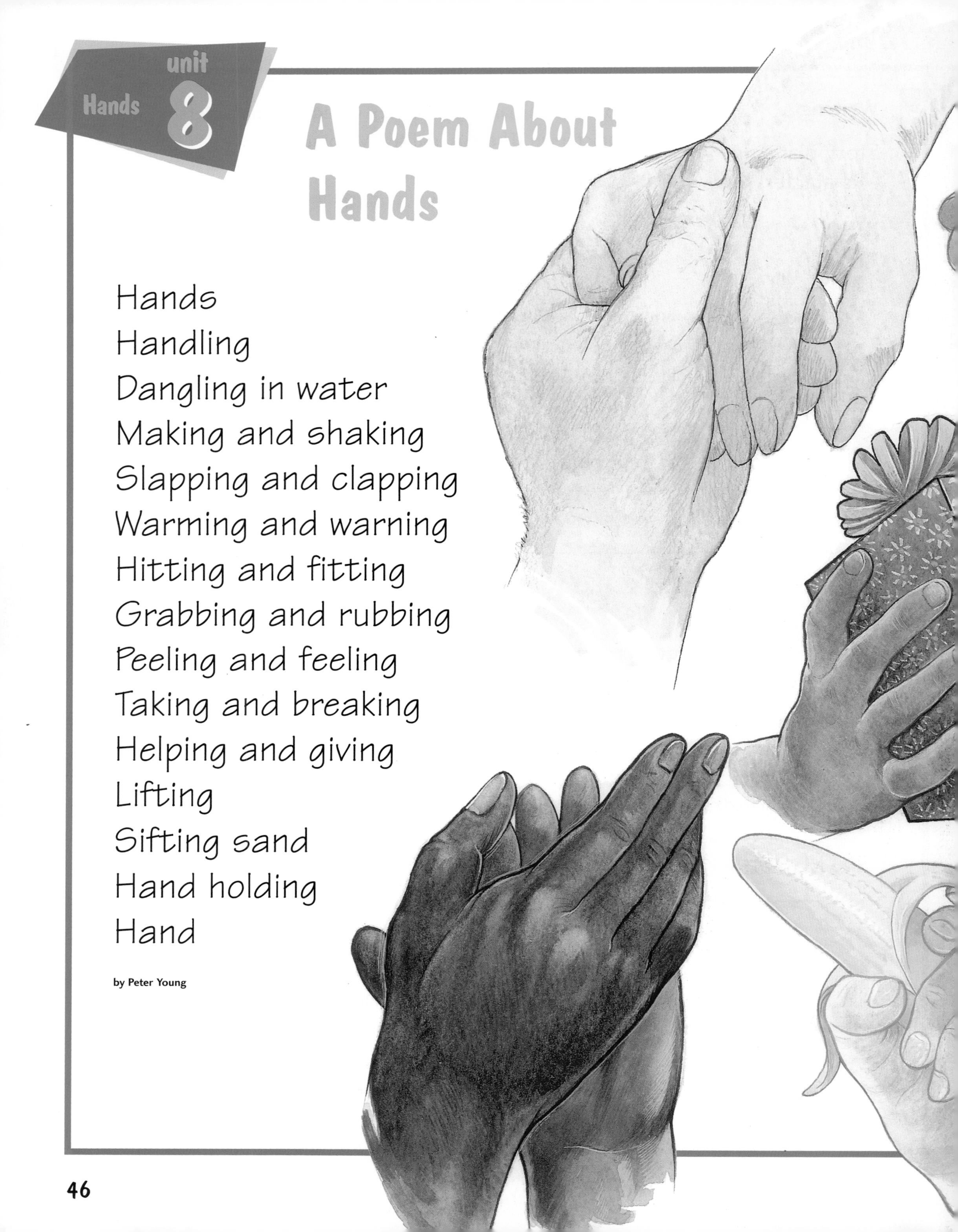

A Poem About Hands

Hands
Handling
Dangling in water
Making and shaking
Slapping and clapping
Warming and warning
Hitting and fitting
Grabbing and rubbing
Peeling and feeling
Taking and breaking
Helping and giving
Lifting
Sifting sand
Hand holding
Hand

by Peter Young

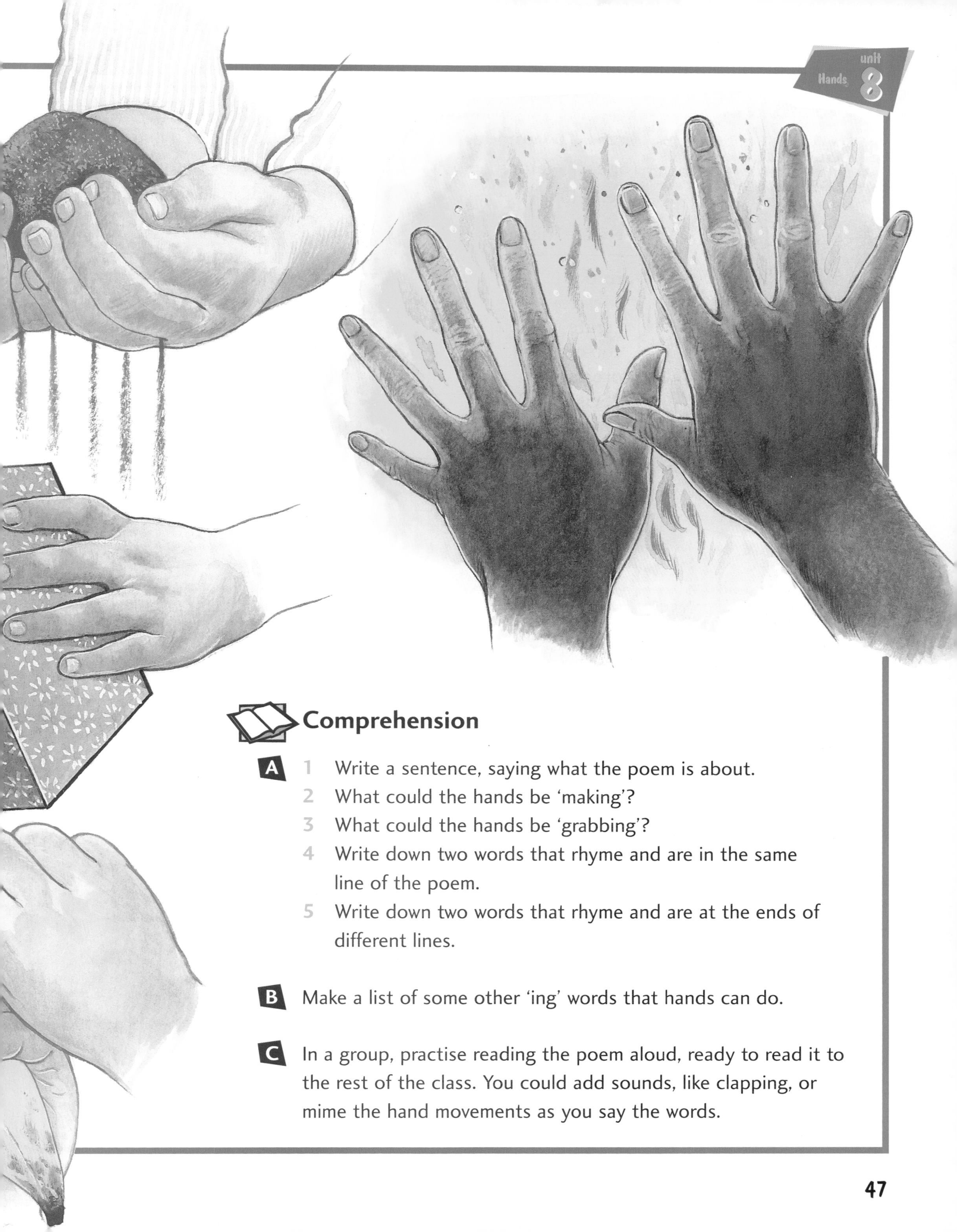

Comprehension

A
1. Write a sentence, saying what the poem is about.
2. What could the hands be 'making'?
3. What could the hands be 'grabbing'?
4. Write down two words that rhyme and are in the same line of the poem.
5. Write down two words that rhyme and are at the ends of different lines.

B Make a list of some other 'ing' words that hands can do.

C In a group, practise reading the poem aloud, ready to read it to the rest of the class. You could add sounds, like clapping, or mime the hand movements as you say the words.

Vocabulary

Using a thesaurus

Remember, the **synonym** of a word means the same thing, or nearly the same. The **antonym** of a word means the opposite.

Remember, a **thesaurus** is a book giving the synonyms of common words. The words are in alphabetical order to help you find them. For each word, there is a list of synonyms, and the antonym, if it has one. A thesaurus might also show other words in the same family.

Here are thesaurus entries for the words 'make', 'shake' and 'warm':

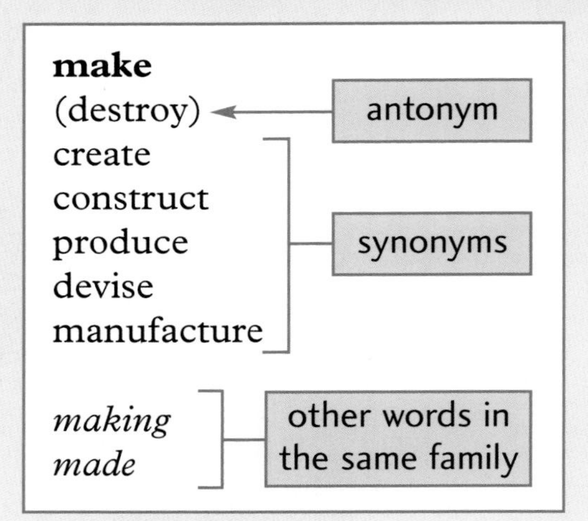

shake
shiver
tremble
shudder
quiver
vibrate

shaky

warm
(cool)
heated
tepid
hot
lukewarm
snug

warmth

A Look at the thesaurus entries above.

1. a Which word beginning with 'd' means 'make'?
   b Which word beginning with 't' means 'shake'?
   c What is the antonym of 'warm'?

2. Copy these sentences. Replace each coloured word with a better one that means that same.

   a When I'm cold, I shake.

   b The hens make tasty, fresh eggs.

   c Mum said the water was only just warm.

Use a thesaurus to help you.

B Write some synonyms for the coloured word in each sentence.

1. I went to help the old man across the icy road.
2. At first, he didn't want to take my help.
3. I was frightened he would fall and break a bone.
4. I managed to grab him as he slipped.

Spelling

Adding 'ing'

Remember, to add 'ing' to a short word, look at the letter before the last letter.
If it isn't a vowel, just add 'ing'.
If it is a single vowel, double the last letter and add 'ing'.
But if the letter before is a vowel too, just add 'ing'. For example:

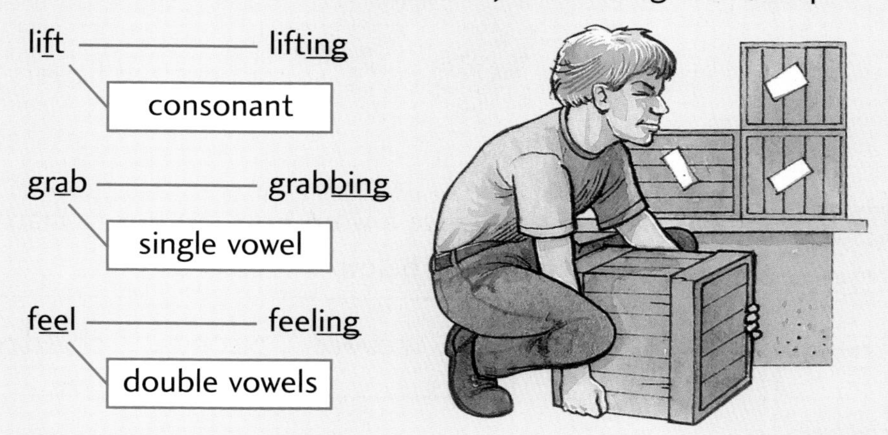

For words ending in w, x or y, **don't** double the last letter. For example:

stay staying

A Add 'ing' to each of these words. The first one has been done to help you.

1 pat patting

2 fit 3 hit 4 rub 5 slip

6 lead 7 grab 8 clap 9 skip

Remember, to add 'ing' to a word that ends with 'e', we usually remove the 'e' and add 'ing'. For example:

make making
live living

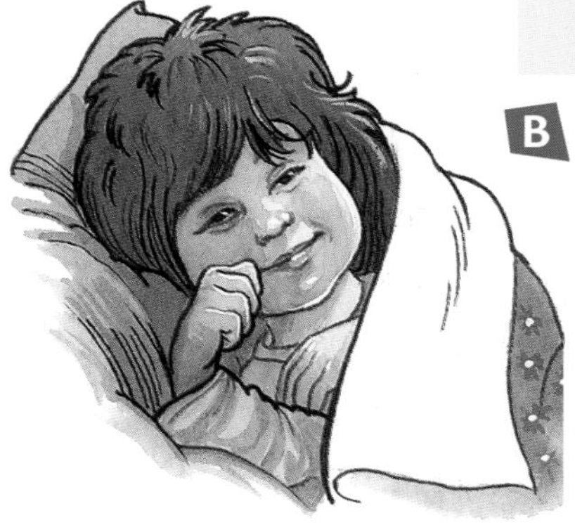

B Add 'ing' to each of these words.

1 wake 2 dangle 3 shake 4 take

5 give 6 slide 7 measure 8 paddle

9 grumble 10 scramble 11 smile 12 tumble

Grammar

Collective nouns

Remember, a **collective noun** is a special name for a group (a 'collection') of people, places or things. For example:

a pack of cards

a bunch of flowers

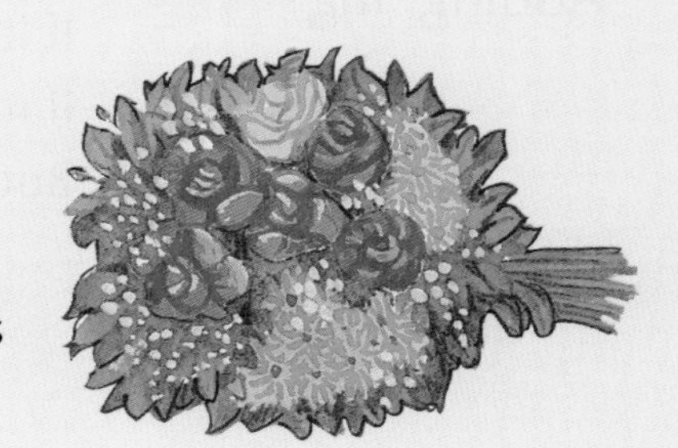

A Choose a word from the box to match each of the collective nouns below.

wolves	puppies	children	ships	birds	bees

1 swarm   2 pack   3 flock
4 litter   5 fleet   6 class

You can use a dictionary to help you.

B What would you expect to find in each of these groups?

1 a team	2 a shoal	3 an army
4 a gaggle	5 a pride	6 an orchestra
7 a bouquet	8 a queue	9 a clutch
10 a suite	11 a regiment	12 a flotilla

Punctuation

Using capital letters

A **capital letter** is often used at the beginning of each new line of a poem. For example:

Making and shaking
Slapping and clapping
Warming and warning

Don't forget the capital letter at the beginning of each line of poetry!

A Copy four lines, or a verse, of a poem that you have read and enjoyed.

B Try to write another verse for the poem yourself.

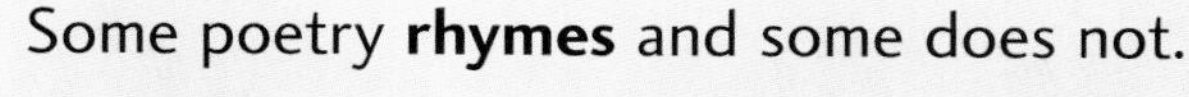

Writing

Poetry – rhyming

Some poetry **rhymes** and some does not.

In lots of poems, the words that rhyme are at the end of lines. For example:

> Jack and <u>Jill</u>
> Went up the <u>hill</u>

Some poems, like 'Hands', have rhyming words in the same lines. For example:

> <u>Peeling</u> and <u>feeling</u>
> <u>Taking</u> and <u>breaking</u>

A 1 Make a list of 'ing' words to describe what your face can do.
For example:
My face can be: grinning

winking

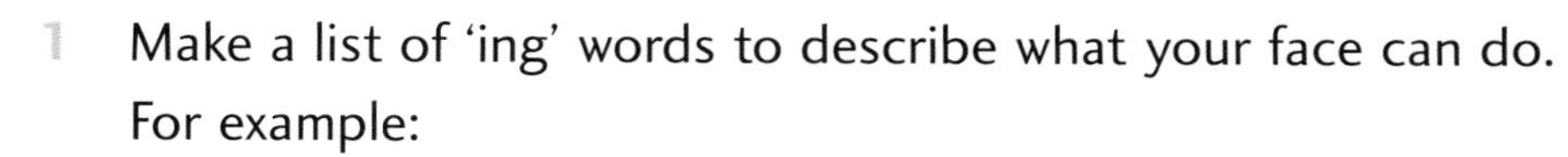

2 Make a list of 'ing' words to describe what your feet can do.
For example:
My feet can be: walking

stamping

B Use your list of 'ing' words from Part A to make up a poem about your face or your feet. Write out your poem in the same way as 'Hands'. Try to use words in the same line that rhyme.

Here are some ways you could begin your poem:

Faces
Faces
Winking
Sleeping in bed

Feet
Feet
Splashing
Stamping in puddles

The Mad Hatter's Tea Party

There was a table set out under a tree in front of the house, and the March Hare and the Hatter were having tea at it; a dormouse was sitting between them, fast asleep, and the other two were using it as a cushion, resting their elbows on it, and talking over its head. "Very uncomfortable for the Dormouse," thought Alice; "only, as it's asleep, I suppose it doesn't mind."

The table was a large one, but the three were all crowded together at one corner of it. "No room! No room!" they cried out when they saw Alice coming.

"There's plenty of room!" said Alice indignantly, and she sat down in a large arm-chair at one end of the table.

"Have some wine," the March Hare said, in an encouraging tone.

Alice looked all round the table, but there was nothing on it but tea. "I don't see any wine," she remarked.

"There isn't any," said the March Hare.

From *Alice's Adventures in Wonderland* by Lewis Carroll

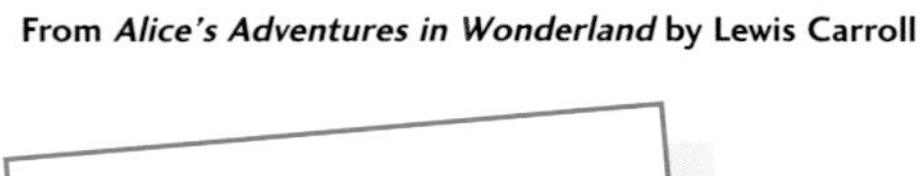

GLOSSARY

indignantly angrily

Comprehension

A Write a sentence to answer each question.

1. Where were the March Hare and the Mad Hatter having tea?
2. Where was the Dormouse?
3. What did the March Hare offer to Alice?
4. Why was this an odd thing to do?

B Think about how the characters behaved.

1. How did the March Hare and the Hatter behave towards the Dormouse?
2. How did the March Hare behave towards Alice?
3. Do you think Alice was right to sit down at the table?
4. What do you think Alice thought about the Mad Hatter and his friends?

C The Mad Hatter's tea party wasn't much of a party! There was only tea to drink and no food! Write a list of the food and drink you think the Mad Hatter should have had at his tea party.

Vocabulary

Synonyms – 'said'

When you are writing dialogue (what people said), you don't have to keep repeating 'said'. There are lots of other words you can use instead of 'said', for example:

asked	shouted	screamed	exclaimed	yelled
called	answered	declared	mumbled	whispered
gasped	muttered	groaned	commented	remarked

These words are all **synonyms** of 'said'. Using synonyms can improve your writing by making it more varied.

Read all the sentences before you start writing!

A Look at the passage 'The Mad Hatter's Tea Party'. Write down the two synonyms that the author has used for 'said'.

B Here are some more sentences from *Alice's Adventures in Wonderland*. Copy each sentence and choose the word from the box that best fits the gap.

asked	replied	pleaded	sighed	inquired

1 "What size do you want to be?" ______ the Caterpillar.

2 "Oh, I'm not particular as to size," Alice ______ .

3 "Oh, please mind what you are doing!" ______ Alice, jumping up and down in an agony of terror.

4 "Two days wrong!" ______ the exasperated Hatter.

5 "What was that?" ______ Alice.

Spelling

Contractions

Contractions are made by leaving out some letters and putting an apostrophe (') in their place.

Remember, a **contraction** is used in place of two words, for example:

"There isn't any," said the March Hare.

"There's plenty of room!" said Alice.

isn't is a contraction for 'is not'.

there's is a contraction for 'there is'.

Here are some more contractions:

I'll = I will   don't = do not   you're = you are

A Choose a contraction from the box for each pair of words.

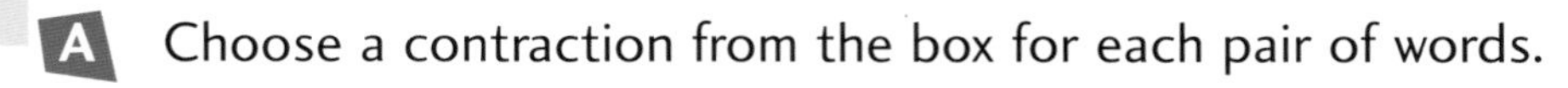

1 she will   2 we would   3 I am
4 you have   5 they are   6 should not

B 1 Write down the contraction for each pair of words.

a shall not   b I have   c they are
d could not   e has not   f we are

2 Copy the sentences below, replacing the pink words with contractions.

a "What is the answer?"

b "I have not the slightest idea!"

c "I will eat it," said Alice.

d "I do not know what you mean," said Alice.

e "Yes, that is it," said the Hatter, "it is always tea time."

Grammar

Pronouns

A **pronoun** can be used in the place of a noun.
Here are some common pronouns:

I you him it she he they

For example:

"Alice will sit next to the Mad Hatter," said the Duchess.

nouns

"You will sit next to him," she said.

pronouns

Remember, a **noun** is the name of a person, place or thing.

A Copy the sentences below. In each sentence, replace the pink words with a pronoun.

1. The March Hare had just upset the milk-jug into his plate.
2. The Dormouse, March Hare and Mad Hatter all seemed very strange to Alice.
3. The Mad Hatter should learn not to make personal remarks," Alice said to the Hatter.

B 1. Copy the first sentence from the passage on page 52. Draw a circle around each pronoun.

2. Write the sentence again, this time putting in the nouns that the pronouns had been used to replace.

Punctuation

Dialogue

Remember, we use **speech marks** (" ") when we write the words that a person actually said. We put a **comma** before the speech marks, at the end of the words spoken, if it is not the end of the whole sentence. For example:

"There isn't any," said the March Hare.

A Copy the sentences below, adding the missing punctuation.

1 I don't care for jam said Alice.

2 It's very good jam said the Queen.

3 Well I don't want any today insisted Alice.

B In the sentences below, all the punctuation marks and capital letters are missing. Copy these sentences, adding the full stops, question marks, capital letters, speech marks and commas that have been left out.

1 tell us a story said the march hare to the dormouse

2 yes please do pleaded alice

3 be quick about it added the hatter

Writing

First and third person

The passage 'The Mad Hatter's Tea Party' is part of a much longer story called *Alice's Adventures in Wonderland.*

The author is not in the story himself. He writes about other characters, so we say the story is written in the **third person**. For example:

Alice looked all around the table.

If Alice had written the story herself, she would have written:

I looked all around the table.

Alice would have been writing in the **first person**.

A Imagine you are Alice in the story. Write about the tea party from your point of view. Begin like this:

I saw a table set out under a tree. The March Hare and the Mad Hatter were sitting at the table.

B Read the passage on page 52 again. Use the third person to write what might happen next in the story. Write what Alice and the March Hare might have said next. The Hatter and the Dormouse can speak as well.

Storms

unit 10

The Cyclone

This is an extract from *The Wizard of Oz*, an amazing adventure story, which begins with a cyclone! The story is about a girl called Dorothy, who lives on a farm in Kansas, USA, with her Uncle Henry and her Aunt Em.

Suddenly Uncle Henry stood up.

"There's a cyclone coming, Em," he called to his wife. "I'll go look after the stock." Then he ran towards the sheds where the cows and horses were kept.

Aunt Em dropped her work and came to the door. One glance told her of the danger close at hand.

"Quick, Dorothy!" she screamed. "Run for the cellar!"

Toto jumped out of Dorothy's arms and hid under the bed, and the girl started to get him. Aunt Em, badly frightened, threw open the trap door in the floor and climbed down the ladder into the small, dark hole. Dorothy caught Toto at last, and started to follow her aunt. When she was halfway across the room there came a great shriek from the wind, and the house shook so hard that she lost her footing and sat down suddenly upon the floor.

A strange thing then happened.

The house whirled around two or three times and rose slowly through the air. Dorothy felt as if she were going up in a balloon.

The north and south winds met where the house stood, and made it the exact centre of the cyclone. In the middle of a cyclone the air is generally still, but the great pressure of the wind on every side of the house raised it up higher and higher, until it was at the very top of the cyclone; and there it remained and was carried miles and miles away as easily as you could carry a feather.

From *The Wizard of Oz* by L Frank Baum

Glossary

cellar a storage area under a house

cyclone a very strong wind

stock farm animals

Comprehension

A Write a sentence to answer each question.

1. What did Uncle Henry do after telling his wife that a cyclone was coming?
2. What did Aunt Em tell Dorothy to do?
3. Why did Dorothy sit down on the floor?
4. What is it like in the middle of a cyclone?
5. What happened to the house?

B

1. Why do you think Uncle Henry went to look after the stock?
2. What do you think Toto is?
3. Why do you think Aunt Em was 'badly frightened'?
4. How do you think Dorothy was feeling?

C Imagine you are Dorothy, in the house as it is being carried 'miles and miles away'. Write about how you would feel.

Vocabulary

Homonyms

Homonyms are words that sound the same and are spelt the same, but which have different meanings. For example:

The house <u>rose</u> slowly through the air.
The man scratched his hand on a <u>rose</u> bush.

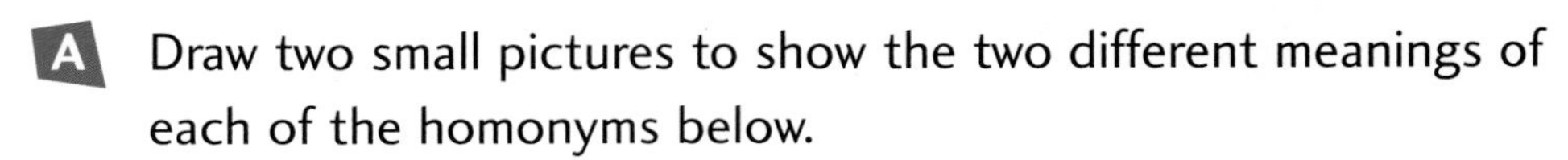

A Draw two small pictures to show the two different meanings of each of the homonyms below.

1 wave 2 rock 3 bank 4 box

Some of the words have more than two different meanings!

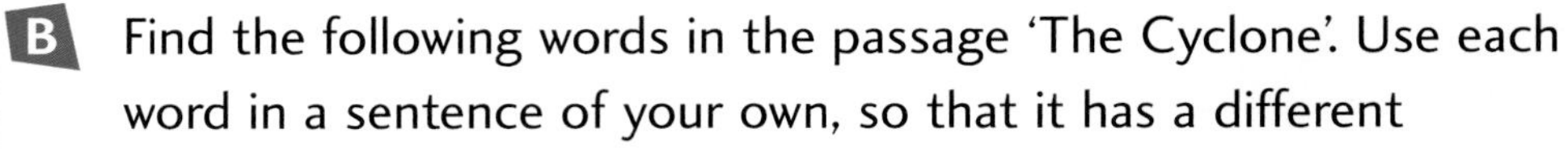

B Find the following words in the passage 'The Cyclone'. Use each word in a sentence of your own, so that it has a different meaning to its meaning in the passage.

1 stock 2 arms 3 trap 4 felt

Spelling

Singular and plural nouns

Remember, when we write about only one thing, it is **singular**.
When we write about two or more things, they are **plural**.
We usually add 's' or 'es' to make a noun plural. For example:

cow + 's' = cow<u>s</u>

We add 'es' if a noun ends with 's', 'x', 'ch' or 'sh'. For example:

dish + 'es' = dish<u>es</u>

A Write the plural of each word.

1 balloon 2 shed 3 bush 4 box
5 parcel 6 flash 7 torch 8 cyclone

When a noun ends in 'y', it is made plural by changing the 'y' to 'i' and adding 'es'. For example:

stor<u>y</u> stor<u>ies</u>

But, if the letter before the 'y' is a vowel, simply add 's'. For example:

to<u>y</u> toy<u>s</u>

B Write the plural of each word.

1 baby 2 day 3 tray 4 hobby
5 motorway 6 valley 7 fly 8 boy

Grammar

Gender words

Gender words tell us whether a person or animal is male or female. For example:

A girl is a female child.
A boy is a male child.

A Copy and complete this table of females and males.

female	male
girl	boy
mother	
grandmother	
	uncle
daughter	
	bull
queen	
	prince

Remember, a **pronoun** is a word that can be used in the place of a noun.

B 1 Copy the pronouns below. Next to each, write M for male, F for female and B if it can be both male and female.

a him b it c she d he
e they f you g her h I

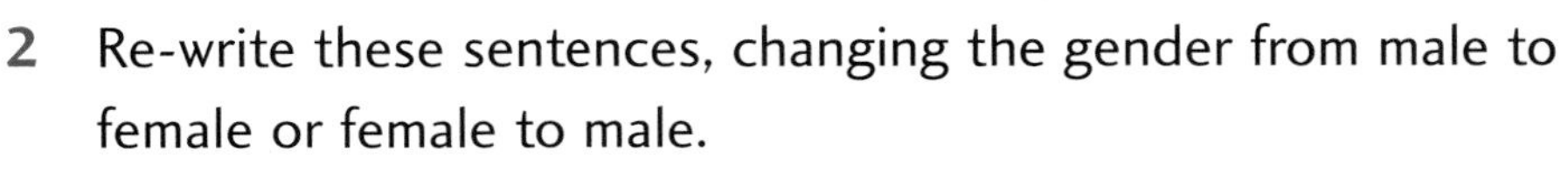

2 Re-write these sentences, changing the gender from male to female or female to male.

a He ran to look after the cows.
b She told her to run for the cellar.
c She picked up Toto in her arms.

Punctuation

Speech marks

Remember, when we write dialogue (what people said), we put **speech marks** around the exact words the person said. The speaker's name usually goes **after** the words that were spoken. For example:

"I really enjoyed reading *The Wizard of Oz*," said Sarah.

Sometimes, the speaker's name comes **before** the words that were spoken. For example:

Sarah said, "I really enjoyed reading *The Wizard of Oz*."

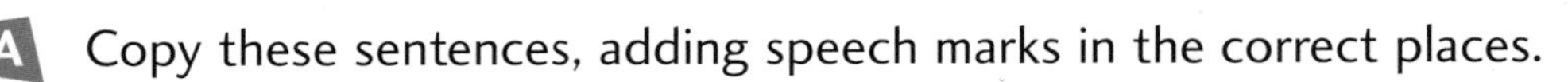

A Copy these sentences, adding speech marks in the correct places.

1. Her friend added, It is the best book I've read.
2. Their teacher said, Would you like me to read it to the class?
3. The class cheered and said, Yes please!
4. Miss Edmunds laughed and said, Well, only if you sit very quietly.

Sometimes, the speaker's name comes in the **middle** of the words that were spoken. For example:

"I know you want to hear the story," said Miss Edmunds, "but you must clear up the classroom first."

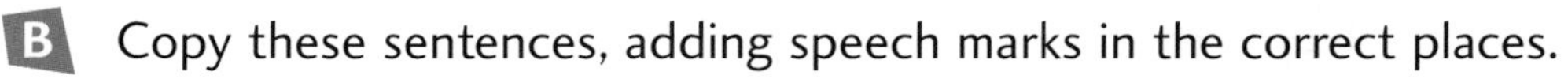

B Copy these sentences, adding speech marks in the correct places.

1. Quick, Dorothy! she screamed. Run for the cellar!
2. Uncle Henry, shouted Dorothy. Be careful!
3. Come here, Toto, called the girl, or you'll get hurt.
4. I'm scared, Aunt Em, said Dorothy. Uncle Henry could be killed.
5. He has to see to the stock, said Aunt Em, and lock it in the barn.

Writing

How stories make you feel

Think about a story you have just finished reading.

- How did you feel when you were reading it?
- What did it feel like when you got to the end of the story?
- Did some parts of the story make you laugh?
- Did you feel frightened, excited, sad?
- Did you like all the characters in the story?
- Did you dislike some of them?

A good story makes you have lots of feelings while you are reading it.

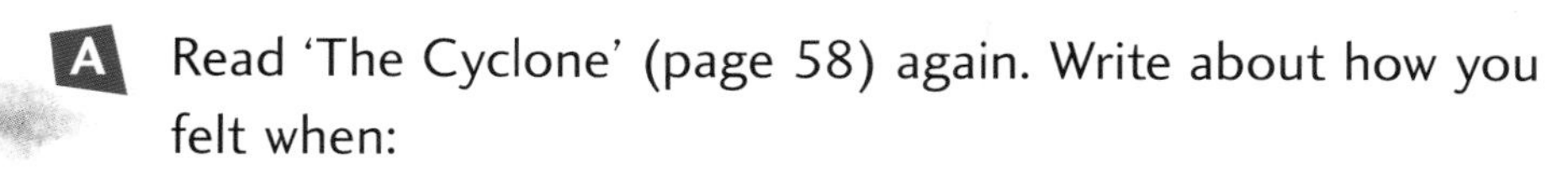

A Read 'The Cyclone' (page 58) again. Write about how you felt when:

1 Uncle Henry said there was a cyclone coming;

2 Aunt Em shrieked;

3 the house shook and Dorothy sat down;

4 the house was raised up by the wind and carried away.

B Think about Aunt Em. Write a sentence or two about Aunt Em in a way that would make the reader:

1 dislike her;

2 frightened of her;

3 laugh.

Book Reviews

A book review gives a reviewer's opinion of the book and usually a brief outline of the plot (story). Book reviews can help you to decide whether or not you would like to read a story book or an information book.

Peter and his friends have played in the deserted garden of 23 Fern Road every Saturday for weeks. No one minds because the house has been empty for years.

One Saturday, however, they discover, to their surprise, that the house isn't there any more! There's number 22 Fern Road and number 24 Fern Road but no number 23!

Peter and his friends set about solving the mystery and meet many amazing characters – some friendly, some frightening – along the way.

For anyone who likes working out clues and solving mysteries, this book will be a very enjoyable read. Both adults and children will find it exciting and will not be able to put it down until the mystery is solved!

Comprehension

A Look at the review of *The Mystery of the Vanishing House.*

1. Who are the main characters in the story?
2. What is the address of the house that vanishes?
3. List the words that describe the characters Peter meets.
4. Who does the reviewer think will enjoy reading the book?

Set in a small African village, *African Adventure* tells the story of a girl called Maya, who makes friends with a wounded lion. The villagers are terrified of the lion and want to kill it but Maya is determined to keep the lion alive.

She sets out on a long journey into the African wilderness to take the lion back to its family.

This book is well written, making the readers feel as if they, too, are travelling with Maya and the lion through the burning African landscape.

Maya faces many adventures and whether she succeeds or fails in her quest is only revealed in the final pages of the book.

Comprehension

B Look at the review of *African Adventure*.

1. What is the setting for the beginning of the story?
2. Who is the main character?
3. What do the villagers want to do to the lion?
4. Why does the reviewer think the book is 'well written'?

C

1. Why do you think the book reviews do not tell you what happens at the end of the story?
2. Which book do you think you would most like to read? Why?

Vocabulary

Homonyms

Remember, **homonyms** are words that sound the same and are spelt the same, but which have different meanings. For example:

Book reviews help us choose what to read.
Mum phoned the cinema to book our tickets.

A Neatly copy this short paragraph, underlining all the homonyms.

The two crooks were hatching a plan to break into the bank. It was a good time, with all the fans milling about on their way to see the match at the local football club. They didn't know that a watch was being kept on them until they heard the police dog bark!

B Choose two homonyms from Part A. Use each in a sentence of your own, to show its different meanings.

Spelling

Root words

Remember, a **prefix** is a group of letters added to the beginning of a word. A **suffix** is a group of letters added to the end of a word. A **root word** is a word to which prefixes and suffixes can be added to make other words in the same family.

For example: viewing, review, viewed, viewer — view

'View' is a root word.

Root words are important in dictionaries. We often need to look for the root word first.

Be careful! Some words may have a prefix and a suffix, or they may have more than one possible prefix or suffix.

A Copy the words below. Next to each, write the root word. The first one has been done to help you.

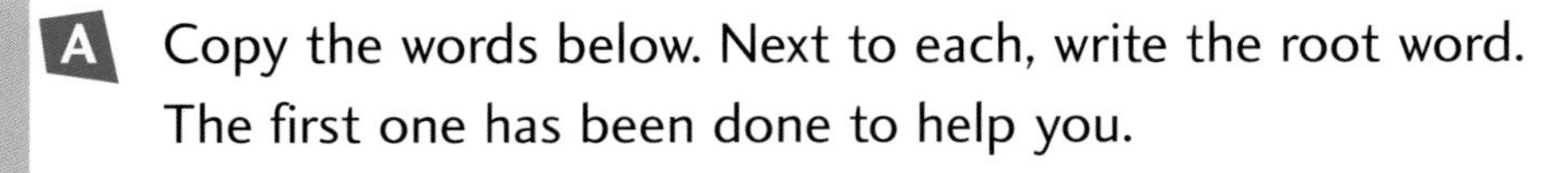

1 working work
2 children
3 villagers
4 unexpected
5 unsolved
6 wilderness
7 jumping
8 unfeeling
9 unsuccessful
10 frightening

Prefixes

un re im

Suffixes

s er ing
ed ly ion
est ness

B 1 See how many words you can make from each root word below. Choose prefixes and suffixes from the boxes. The first one has been done to help you.

a happy unhappy unhappily happier
happily happiest happiness

b mark c tall d invent e dark

2 Choose one of the root words from question 1. Make up a silly sentence using as many of its family words as you can. For example:

The inventor invented an invention to invent inventions.

Grammar

Using 'was' and 'were'

We use 'was' when we write about the actions of **one** person or thing. For example:

Tim was working in the library.

We use 'were' when we write about the actions of **more than one** person or thing. For example:

Tim and Annie were working in the library.

'Were' is also used with 'you', whether the sentence is about one person or more than one person. For example:

"I knew **you** were working in the library," I said to Tim and Annie.

"**You** were helping me with maths, weren't you?" Tim said to Annie.

A Write down whether 'was' or 'were' should go in each numbered gap. The first one has been done to help you.

It 1 was a cold, wet breaktime. We ___2___ allowed to stay indoors and read. I ___3___ sure I had left my book on my desk, but my two friends ___4___ sure I hadn't.
"Where ___5___ you when you last had it?" asked Miss Potts.
"I'm sure I ___6___ at my table," I replied.

B Copy and complete these sentences in any way you wish.

1 I was … 2 You were … 3 We were …

Sentence construction

Conjunctions

Conjunctions are sometimes called 'joining words'.

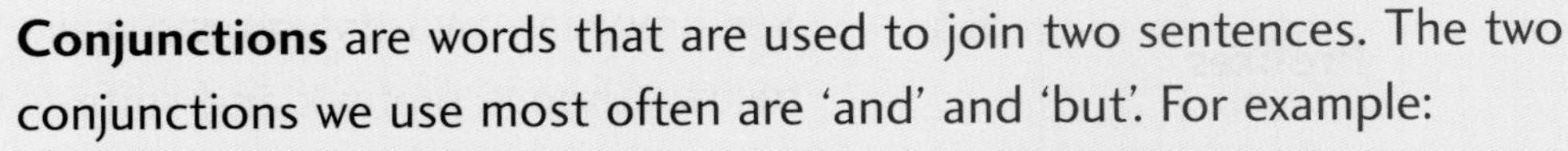

Conjunctions are words that are used to join two sentences. The two conjunctions we use most often are 'and' and 'but'. For example:

I have just been given this book. I am really enjoying it.
I have just been given this book <u>and</u> I am really enjoying it.

I enjoyed this book. I didn't like this one.
I enjoyed this book <u>but</u> I didn't like this one.

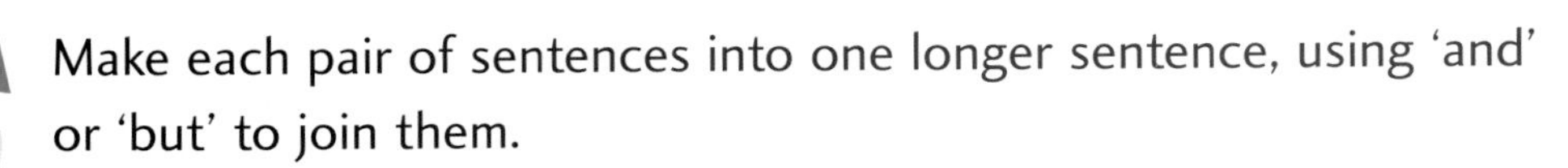

A Make each pair of sentences into one longer sentence, using 'and' or 'but' to join them.

1 I borrowed a book. I read it the same day.

2 I like mystery stories. I don't like stories about sport.

B Write the two shorter sentences that each of these long sentences was made from.

1 I help to keep our library tidy and I write down which books people borrow.

2 Winston wanted to help me but our teacher said we would talk too much.

Writing

Book covers, blurbs and reviews

You can find out a lot about a book by looking at the **cover**. You will find the book title and the author's name on the front cover.

A 1 Write the title and author's name of each of the books below.

2 Write one or two sentences to describe the likely setting for each book.

A young girl is going to visit her old, sick grandmother. Little does she know that it is not her grandmother she will find in the cottage, but someone who wants to eat her!

You may find more information about the book or the author on the back cover. This is called a '**blurb**'. The blurb tells you enough to make you want to read the book, but not too much about what happens.

3 a On the left is a book blurb for *Little Red Riding Hood*. Write in your own words what the 'blurb' has told you.

b What has the blurb not told you? What will you have to read the book to find out?

Book reviews are written by reviewers and you can find them in newspapers and magazines. A reviewer's job is to say what they thought of the book. They give their own opinion. Sometimes, reviewers say a book is very good. Sometimes they say a book is awful! You have to read the book yourself to see whether you agree with the reviewer.

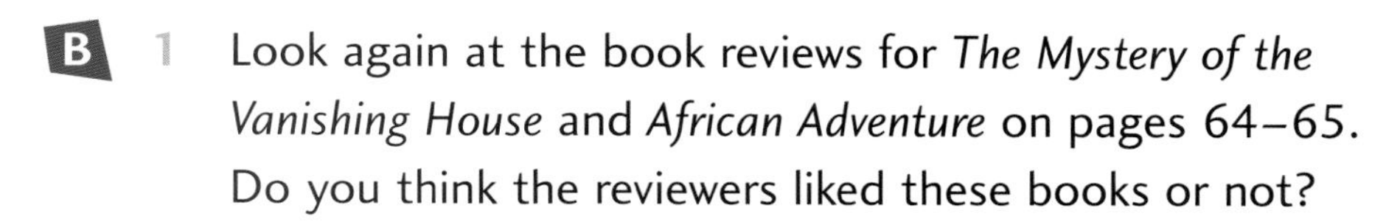

B 1 Look again at the book reviews for *The Mystery of the Vanishing House* and *African Adventure* on pages 64–65. Do you think the reviewers liked these books or not?

2 Write a book review for a story book you have recently read. Remember:

- give the title and author;
- write a little about the story but don't give away the ending;
- write your opinion, saying why you liked or did not like the book.

Tea

unit 12

I'd Like to be a Teabag

I'd like to be a teabag,
And stay at home all day –
And talk to other teabags
In a teabag sort of way ...

I'd love to be a teabag,
And lie in a little box –
And never have to wash my face
Or change my dirty socks ...

I'd like to be a teabag,
An Earl Grey one perhaps,
And doze all day and lie around
With Earl Grey kind of chaps.

I wouldn't have to do a thing,
No homework, jobs or chores –
Comfy in my caddy
Of teabags and their snores.

I wouldn't have to do exams,
I needn't tidy rooms,
Or sweep the floor or feed the cat
Or wash up all the spoons.

I wouldn't have to do a thing,
A life of bliss – you see . . .
Except that once in all my life

I'd make a cup of tea!

by Peter Dixon

Comprehension

A Write a sentence for each answer.

1. What does the first verse say a teabag does?
2. What does the poet want to do in the second verse?
3. Make a list of the things the poet would not have to do if he were a teabag.

B Use a dictionary to find the definitions of these words from the poem:

1 chores 2 caddy 3 bliss

C

1. The poet thinks it would be great to be a teabag. Make a list of things you would not like about being a teabag.
2. Did you find the poem funny? Explain why.

Vocabulary

Synonyms

Synonyms can be very important and useful for poets. For example:

I'd <u>like</u> to be a teabag.

I'd <u>love</u> to be a teabag.

Use a dictionary to check the meaning of any words that you are unsure about.

A Write down the headings 'love' 'talk' and 'eat'. Write each word from the box under the correct heading.

gobble	gossip	devour	like	feed
chatter	esteem	mumble	munch	cherish
express	admire	nibble	speak	chew
articulate	treasure	adore		

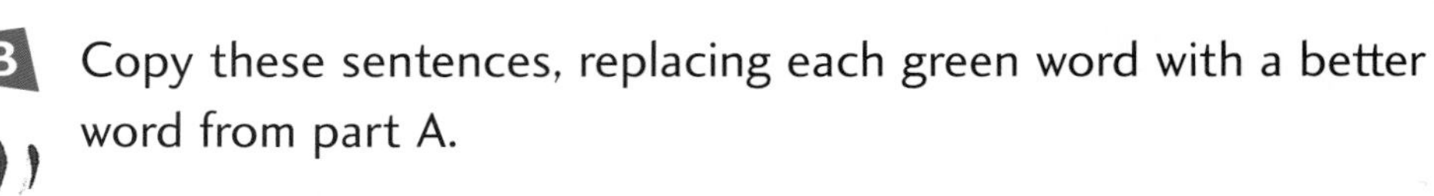

B Copy these sentences, replacing each green word with a better word from part A.

1 The dog settled down to eat its bone.
2 He told the boy not to eat his food in such a disgusting way.
3 It's unkind to talk about someone behind their back.
4 When you talk with your hand over your mouth I can't hear you.
5 The children love their new baby brother.
6 I'll always love the watch my grandfather gave me.

Spelling

Rhyming patterns

Listening and looking for **rhyming patterns** can help with your spelling. For example:

d<u>ay</u>	w<u>ay</u>
perh<u>aps</u>	ch<u>aps</u>

A Write down the answers to the following clues.

1. Something horses eat, which rhymes with 'day'.
2. Something that is used for making pottery, which rhymes with 'way'.
3. These are set to catch mice and rats, and rhyme with 'perhaps'.
4. These help us to find our way around, and rhyme with 'chaps'.
5. This is the middle of an apple, and rhymes with 'snore'.
6. This is the opposite of 'after', and rhymes with 'chore'.

B Write four more words that have the same spelling pattern as each word below. The first one has been done to help you.

1 clown down brown town gown

2 cold 3 fine 4 catch 5 bread

Grammar

Pronouns and contractions

Remember, a **pronoun** can be used in place of a noun. For example:

Liam likes a cup of tea. <u>He</u> likes a cup of tea.

A **contraction** is used in place of two words. For example:

He is drinking his tea. <u>He's</u> drinking his tea.

A Many pronouns are used in contractions. Copy each pair of words below, and underline the pronoun, then write a contraction next to the pair. The first has been done to help you.

1 he is <u>he</u> is he's

2 she will 3 I am 4 he will 5 they are

B Look through your reading book and make a list of all the contractions you can find. Then, draw a circle around all the contractions that contain pronouns.

Sentence construction

Order and time words

Some words are useful when we are writing about things that happen in a set order. For example:

To make a cup of tea, first fill a kettle. Then put the kettle on to boil while you get the teapot.

Here are some other useful order and time words:

second	third	fourth	next	after
meanwhile	from	when	now	

Never boil a kettle without the help of an adult.

A Look at the pictures below. Write a sentence to go with each picture, so that they make instructions about how to make a cup of tea. Underline the time and order words that you use.

B Think about the stages of clearing the table and washing up after a meal. Write a series of short sentences describing the order in which things need to be done. Underline the time and order words that you use.

Writing

Humorous poetry

Humorous poetry makes us smile or laugh out loud. It is funny. Sometimes it is about a funny person. Sometimes it is about a funny event or situation. One type of funny poem is a **limerick**. For example:

There was a young lady from Ickenham
Who went on a bus trip to Twickenham.
She ate too much cake
Which made her tummy ache
So she took off her boots and was sick in 'em.

A Do you think the limerick above is funny? Explain why.

Limericks always have five lines: lines 1, 2 and 5 rhyme
lines 3 and 4 rhyme.

B 1 Read again the limerick about the girl from Ickenham. Copy and complete this table.

Line:	Rhyming word:	Line:	Rhyming word:
1		3	
2		4	
5			

2 Write your own limerick. You could complete the half-finished limerick below, or make up one yourself.

There was a young man from Crewe
Who thought ______________________ .
When he ______________________
He ______________________
And ______________________ .

Think of lots of words that rhyme with 'Crewe' before you start!

Check-up

Check-up

Vocabulary

A Copy these sentences. Fill each gap by choosing from the box the **synonym** of the coloured word.

dirty picked feel shove throw

1 Touch the cup, and ______ how hot it is.

2 Line up quietly, and don't push and ______ other children.

3 Toss the coin, but don't ______ it too high

4 I chose sausages, but Ali ______ a meat pie for his lunch.

5 Sam fell in the muddy puddle and made his coat all ______.

B Use each pair of **synonyms** below in a sentence of your own.

1 closed shut 2 cool chilly 3 angry cross 4 miserable sad

C Make a list of six **synonyms** that might be used instead of 'said' when writing direct speech.

D Find and write down each pair of **antonyms** from the box.

heavy big difficult beautiful fast asleep
easy slow small awake ugly light

E Use each of the **homonyms** below in two sentences of your own, to show that it can have different meanings.

1 back 2 cross 3 show 4 trip

F Write these words in **alphabetical order**.

asked shouted yelled screamed declared mumbled answered

Spelling

A Add the **prefix** 'un' to each word, then write the meaning of the new word.

1 tie 2 happy 3 sure 4 believable
5 even 6 safe 7 true 8 fair

B Write three more words that have the same spelling pattern as each of the words below.

1 mine 2 sight 3 pile 4 crow
5 brown 6 thrown 7 how 8 kite

C Each of these words has a **silent letter** that has been missed out. Write the words correctly, adding the missing letters.

1 nee 2 nock 3 lam 4 thisle
5 rite 6 bom 6 wistle 8 crum

D Write a **contraction** for each pair of words.

1 it is 2 I will 3 we are 4 you would
5 shall not 6 would not 7 there is 8 we will

E Write the **plural** of each of these words.

1 mat 2 bush 3 torch 4 ditch
5 box 6 baby 7 trolley 8 spy

F Add '**ing**' to each of these words.

1 hop 2 jump 3 sing 4 rip
5 clap 6 live 7 paddle 8 fiddle

Grammar

A Copy these sentences and underline the **verbs**.

1 William ran to school.
2 The lorry delivered the furniture.
3 The woodcutter's wife cried.
4 The snow fell on the trees.

B Rewrite these sentences so that they describe events that happened in the **past**.

1 I hold my coat over my head.
2 I swim in the waves.
3 I play rounders with my friends.
4 I sit and work at my computer.

C Copy each sentence, using '**was**' or '**were**' to fill the gap.

1 William ______ upset to be moved from his bedroom.
2 Hansel and Gretel ______ left in the wood.
3 Leon thought he ______ the best footballer in his class.
4 How old ______ you last birthday?
5 His grandparents said they ______ coming to stay for Christmas.

D Add another word to each word below, to make a **compound noun**.

1 day 2 post 3 snow 4 foot 5 milk

E Match each word below with the correct **collective noun** from the box.

team	flock
forest	gaggle
herd	shoal

1 cows 2 netball players 3 geese
4 fish 5 trees 6 birds

F Write two **adjectives** that could be used to describe each of the following.

1 a tomato 2 a mouse 3 a fire 4 snow

G Copy this sentence and underline the three **pronouns**.

It was a hot day when they went to see her in hospital.

Check-up

Punctuation

Check-up

A Copy each sentence, adding the missing **punctuation** mark at the end.

1 William loved his room
2 Can we buy some food
3 What can we do
4 It is my birthday tomorrow
5 Help
6 Ouch, that hurt

B Copy these sentences, adding the missing **commas.**

1 The snake monkey zebra birds and giraffe watched the tug-of-war.
2 There was a big house a small house a short house a tall house a long house a red house a blue house and a white house.
3 "Come home early" called his Mum.
4 "I will" he replied.

C Copy these sentences, adding the missing **speech marks.**

1 I like adventure stories, said James.
2 So do I, agreed Jenny.
3 If you look after it, said James, you can read my book.
4 Thank you, replied his sister. I will be very careful with it.

D Neatly copy the paragraph below into your book, adding the missing **punctuation** and **capital letters.**

rupert and his friends vinod hansa and kim were playing in the garden. suddenly they heard a scream. did you hear that asked kim it came from the other side of the fence said hansa. help help please come and help called mrs jackson. ive fallen over and i may have broken my leg please come quickly she shouted quick said rupert i'll get help while you all go and look after her.

Writing

Story writing

1. Plan a story called 'An Amazing Adventure'. Think about what will happen:
   - at the beginning of your story
   - in the middle of your story
   - at the end of your story.
2. Make notes on two important characters in your story. Think about:
   - what each character looks like
   - what sort of person each character is.
3. Write the opening of your story. Do you want your reader to:
   - feel frightened?
   - feel sad?
   - laugh?

   Begin your story in one of these ways:
   - by describing the setting
   - by describing the characters
   - with a conversation.

Book covers

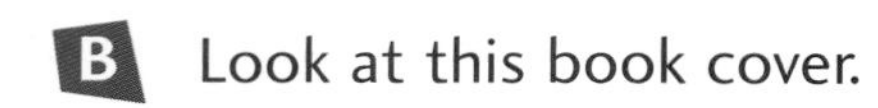

B Look at this book cover.

What do you think the story could be about?

Write a blurb to go on the back cover.

Playscripts

C Choose a part of your favourite story in which two characters are talking to each other. Write their conversation as a playscript.